Investigating Drama

Investigating Drama

Kenneth Pickering

with Bill Horrocks and David Male

Illustrations by Margaret Maisey

London   George Allen & Unwin Ltd
Ruskin House   Museum Street

First published in 1974

© George Allen & Unwin Ltd 1974

ISBN 0 04 372011 0

Printed in Great Britain
in 11 point Times Roman type by
Cox & Wyman Ltd, London, Fakenham and Reading

Acknowledgements

Grateful acknowledgement for permission to reproduce copyright material is made to: Heinemann Educational Books Ltd for the extract from *A Man for all Seasons* by Robert Bolt; David Higham Associates Ltd and Faber & Faber Ltd for the scene from *Luther* by John Osborne; Methuen & Co. Ltd for extracts from *Mother Courage* by Bertolt Brecht, translated by Eric Bentley; Faber & Faber Ltd for 'Interlude'—the Archbishop's sermon from *Murder in the Cathedral* by T. S. Eliot, for the extract from *The Film Sense* by Sergei Eisenstein and for W. H. Auden's poem 'O What is that Sound?'; Maurice Temple Smith Ltd for the quotation from *Brief Chronicles* by Martin Esslin; *Radio Times* for the feature '*Elizabeth R*'; *Theatre Quarterly* for extracts from Peter Weiss's article on documentary drama; Thames Television and author Michael Cahill for the extract from *You and the World*; the *Daily Telegraph* for Eric Shorter's article; and Avice Allchin, Kent County Drama Inspector, for articles from *Vox*.

We also wish to express our sincere thanks to: David Campton, Douglas Walters, Joan Charlton and Cathy Haines for their invaluable contributions; the Marlowe Theatre, Canterbury, and Rank Strand Electrics; Aneurin John, Architect of the London Borough of Bromley; Rodney Wood and John Howell at Hereford College of Education for some of the original inspiration and Fiona Bavestock for her work on the original drafts; finally, for their continued help throughout the project, Susan ffitch, Irene Pickering and our editor Patrick Gallagher.

Sittingbourne College of Education, Kent   K.W.P.
1973   W.G.H.
       D.A.M.

Contents

Acknowledgements   *page*   7

Introduction   11

Unit 1   Some Vital Questions   15
Unit 2   'O What is that Sound?'   20
Unit 3   The Stage   25
Unit 4   Some Consequences   30
Unit 5   Improvisation   39
Unit 6   'Uneasy Lies the Head'   47
Unit 7   Improvisation: *The Death of Grass*   58
Unit 8   'Let Her Paint an Inch Thick!'   60
Unit 9   'Let There Be Light'—an Act of Creation!   64
Unit 10   Design for the Theatre   71
Unit 11   A Case Study   81
Unit 12   *In Committee*   87
Unit 13   The Director   100
Unit 14   The Stage Manager   104
Unit 15   Documentary Drama   107
Unit 16   Brecht and a History Play?   112
Unit 17   Television: Techniques of Production   118
Unit 18   The Programme in Production   126
Unit 19   Full, Frontal . . .   140
Unit 20   'Though Our Lives . . .'?   144

Glossary of Theatrical Terms   146

Introduction

By the time a pupil has reached the upper stages of the secondary school or a further education establishment, his experience of drama may have consisted of a well-developed course with real involvement, a fringe activity of steadily diminishing interest or downright boredom. Faced with such variety of previous experience, the teacher may find it difficult to decide how drama can be tackled as a worthwhile and rewarding activity with these older pupils or students.

The teacher will also be aware of the almost bewildering variety of theories associated with drama. The majority stress the need for active participation, whilst fewer are concerned with what is often referred to as 'theatre'. The chief difference between them is neatly defined by Brian Way in *Development Through Drama*:

> 'Theatre' is largely concerned with communication between actors and an audience; 'drama' is largely concerned with *experience* by the participants, irrespective of any function of communication.
>
> (page 3)

It can be seen that the second part of the definition describes drama as a participatory activity and emphasises individual experience. It has no particular concern with presentation or performance. Much of that experience will consist of improvisation which stimulates the imagination and encourages its expression in physical and vocal terms. 'Theatre', Way suggests, is concerned with actors performing plays to audiences and so far as the majority of children are concerned is of comparatively minor importance. The passive role as spectator is made to contrast very vividly with improvisation, sensitivity, social drama.

Perhaps it is not necessary to make such severe distinctions. Drama has always been a complex art combining in its more sophisticated forms speech and singing, writing, painting, design and music together with the skills of action in movement or dance, vocalisation in word and song, acting, improvisation, production and presentation. Material for drama is derived from original inspiration, literary and historic sources or eye-catching contemporary events, and offered in a variety of forms—play, dance, ballet, opera, musical, documentary, 'happening'. The results may be seen in classroom, studio, school hall and theatre or on television.

The complexity is also reflected by the many differing contributions that go towards the successful presentation of a play. The traditional priority of producer and actors followed at some distance by designers, stage crew, lighting operator or poster designer is not necessarily to be defended or maintained. Each of these activities will have its own characteristics and its own unique opportunities for investigation, experience and active involvement. The poster design, for example, is allied to the world of art and lithography as well as being specifically concerned with a particular production. Improvisation can exist as a perfectly satisfactory self-supporting activity, yet also provide vital experience in the understanding of a play text.

The aim of this book is to provide an opportunity for investigating drama by a series of units, each of which examines an aspect of drama or theatre. There are opportunities for participation, discussion, research and practical experiment. To this end, no unit should be considered as complete but each should be regarded as an open-ended introduction with suggestions that the pupils or students may follow up. It is not suggested that the book should be studied in the unit sequence. The relationship between certain groups of activities will be obvious, but the particular situation of the teacher may require the exclusion of some units because of inadequate equipment or facilities.

Viewed as a whole, the units will reveal an overall pattern

that deals with theories of acting and the stage and improvisation; production, design, lighting, make-up; study of
play texts and poetry; documentary drama and television.
The brevity of each unit indicates that it is not meant to be
exclusive or comprehensive. The discussion and activity
suggestions often go well beyond the actual content of the
unit. A bibliography is included at the end of each both for
information and as an indication of the need for further
investigation. The units are not intended as lessons but as
projects for investigation. The teacher or tutor may well
decide to use a part of one unit or include a unit in some
more comprehensive study of his own.

It is assumed that the teacher will have some experience
of drama, but may be faced with a group of pupils with no
specialist interest or expertise in the subject. He may be
concerned with including drama in a course of liberal or
aesthetic studies. It is possible to study the units by a practical, active approach, but equally, the work may be chiefly
discussion, research, theatre visiting. If practical work is
possible it will most conveniently take place in a room,
studio or hall with clear floor space where rostra, screens,
lighting, wardrobe and make-up equipment are available.
Participants should be encouraged to wear suitable clothing
and footwear. As soon as is possible, students should be
encouraged to make a study of the apparatus available
(however limited it may be) and learn to use it sensibly and
imaginatively. Certain of the units are specifically directed
towards this essential experience.

Where no practical facilities are available, the teacher
must ensure that an adequate supply of texts, reference
books and other material is available together with some
means of display. It is frequently suggested that collections
of cuttings, pictures, posters etc. are made and there must
be an opportunity to display the result of these investiga-
tions. It is assumed that a high standard of display will be
expected so that the work can be shown to be worth serious
attention and encourage discussion and interest outside the
group.

It is vital that the activity includes theatre visits of some
kind. Even if not all members can attend, the contributions

arising from individual visits should be given attention. Where no theatre visits are possible, the common agreement to view a particular television play or programme could be substituted. Tutors may be able to arrange films related to the theatre or theatrical productions.

Examples have been taken almost indiscriminately from classical and contemporary drama. No attempt has been made to define or illustrate a 'good' play. The hope is that following some acquaintance with the elements of drama, particularly by active participation, the students may bring a more informed and understanding attitude towards drama and the theatre.

NOTE

Investigating Drama is not intended to be simply a school textbook with a series of exercises, or a teacher's guide, but rather a means of focusing attention on aspects of drama which both teacher and pupil can share equally. A deliberately 'low key' style of discussion has been adopted to allow students of a very wide age range to respond to the suggestions and to enable the teacher to provide the particular impetus that his own teaching situation requires. It is hoped that the books listed in the bibliographies will be helpful to teacher and pupil alike.

BIBLIOGRAPHY

G. Barnfield: *Creative Drama in Schools*, Macmillan, London, 1968.
David Male: *Approaches to Drama*, Allen & Unwin, London, 1973.
R. Pemberton Billing and J. D. Clegg: *Teaching Drama*, ULP, London, 1968.
Brian Way: *Development Through Drama*, Longmans, London, 1967.

Unit 1

Some Vital Questions

The word 'dramatic' is often used in our daily lives to describe some exciting or unusual event. A radio or television commentator at a great diplomatic or sporting event may employ such phrases as 'the scene is set' or 'it's a great show' as if he were present at a theatrical performance. There are some important occasions such as weddings, burials, parties and discotheques where we are, perhaps, aware of 'acting a certain part'.

The preparations for a traditional wedding involve careful planning of elaborate costumes; the bride and bridesmaids wear specially designed dresses which must blend with an overall colour scheme reflected in the flowers they carry; men may hire clothes of a type they would never wear in normal life; even the families and guests expend considerable energy and money in ensuring that everyone 'looks the part'.

The ceremony begins at a fixed time; as the guests arrive at the church they are often handed a programme-like 'Order of Service' and ushered to their seats by sidesmen, while the best man ensures (like a good stage manager) that the ring is ready and the bridegroom prepared for his part in the action.

Final touches of make-up and décor are applied before the bride leaves home but her dramatic entrance to the church is a sign that the climax is approaching. She enters and leaves in procession to fanfare-style music: the 'Bridal March' from Wagner's opera *Lohengrin* and 'The Wedding March' from Mendelssohn's music for *A Midsummer Night's Dream* are the most popular pieces. Everyone now has a clearly defined role and an allotted place both in the processions and at the front of the church. The marriage itself may take place on a raised platform while the congregation watches as an audience; nothing is left to chance: there is a script for the main characters, although it is not unknown for nervous brides to need prompting! A series of symbolic actions accompanies the elaborate formal language—for example rings are exchanged with great ceremony between two people who would normally give each other presents in a relaxed and casual manner. Many clergymen insist on a rehearsal of the service to ensure that there are no mistakes.

The service completed, extra sound-effects—peals of bells —may be added; more symbolic acts follow, confetti is thrown, horse-shoes and wooden spoons are offered while carefully staged photographs are taken. The photographer directs every move at this point, including the bride's kisses!

When it is all over a tired mother may be heard to remark 'What a performance!'

A discotheque or dance may take place in darkness broken only by theatrical lighting effects; spotlights, flashing and psychedelic lanterns help to create an atmosphere. As the dancers move, their bodies, now coloured, now in shadow, are the centre of interest; the right clothes are therefore very important. If there is a 'live' group the dancers become, like the congregation at the wedding, both audience and actors. The music throbs away; it is not enough for it just to be audible; spectacular effect involves maximum volume and extravagant gestures. The words of the songs and the patter of the disc jockey may bear little resemblance to everyday speech; the group probably has a 'stage' name. This is the 'pop scene'.

At first sight these descriptions may seem remote from investigating drama, yet the sociologist Goffman once described all social behaviour as a type of drama which involves a 'performance' in front of others (although he suggested that there are some 'off-stage moments'). We talk of 'showing off' or 'putting on an act' to suggest how some people behave in company. The word 'dramatic' is applied to a particularly exciting rescue or sudden catastrophe as well as describing activities concerned with the theatre.

Are some situations more 'dramatic' than others and what qualities make them so? Or do we use the word 'drama' in a series of totally unrelated ways?

These questions will be investigated throughout this project and the experiences that result from following the suggestions may help to clarify your understanding of what is meant by drama.

The first and most vital point about all work in drama is that it is a cooperative activity; you will, therefore, have to work closely with other people, you will get to know them well and your behaviour will be exposed to their critical eye. You may feel apprehensive about making suggestions or doing something in front of others. The prospect probably seems daunting but the experience may benefit you in unexpected ways and will help to deepen your sympathy for and knowledge of humanity.

DISCUSSION AND ACTIVITY

1. In the description of the wedding and the pop scene certain elements of drama or the dramatic were suggested. Search for further examples of events or occasions that in some way resemble a play. You will probably look for a specialised location such as an arena, some kind of organised action, costumed participants performing in a particular way being watched by spectators who understand and occasionally may become involved in the whole situation. (Sporting events, processions, religious ceremonies, competitions, political meetings may prove useful areas of investigation.) Try to decide what the activities have in common and how the words 'drama' and 'dramatic' apply to them. Notice how frequently those words are used in a newspaper headline or magazine article.

2. In Willis Hall's play *The Long and the Short and the Tall* a group of British soldiers find themselves in a hut in the Malayan jungle in 1942 cut off from help by the advancing Japanese army. The danger of the situation and the fact that the men are of differing ranks causes an electric atmosphere;

but worse is to come when they capture a lone Japanese soldier who immediately sets off a series of conflicting reactions. Surprisingly Bamforth, a Cockney blasphemer with a complete contempt for authority, emerges as the only man ready to spare the prisoner's life, whereas the corporal shows a startling degree of sadism. The story is all too familiar when we consider the rumours which have filtered through from Vietnam.

Divide into groups of about six; make a small circle of chairs to represent some confined space and make up a short scene showing a group of people existing there. Use speech only if you wish. Take about ten minutes for discussion and rehearsal.

Did tensions arise in your imagined scene? If so, did these comprise the points which made the scene dramatic?

Did your scene have a clear beginning and ending—if not try to evolve one now? Does the scene now come closer to what you would consider 'dramatic'?

Particular stresses are caused when people are confined together; the strategies which are usually employed in our personal relationships begin to seem inadequate as individuals are unable to escape.

A type of group relationship with its dominant and subservient members usually emerges in the situation we are considering but when there are difficult decisions to make the strains are enormous. When an outsider is added to an already established group another shift of sympathies becomes inevitable.

An interesting follow-up to your improvisations and a reading of Willis Hall's play might be a study of Jean-Paul Sartre's play *In Camera* which demonstrates how other people's presence can become a hell. Intriguing tensions also arise in Harold Pinter's *The Dumb Waiter* as unexpected intrusions disturb two assassins waiting for their victim.

The theme has been explored in a recent TV series *No Exit* and is developed again in Unit 11 when we consider Campton's play *The Cage Birds*.

BIBLIOGRAPHY

Brian Clark: *Group Theatre*, Pitman, London, 1971. For a consideration of working in groups.

Michael Argyle: *The Psychology of Interpersonal Behaviour*, Penguin, Harmondsworth, 1967. For a study of human group behaviour.

Peter R. Newman: *Yesterday's Enemy*, Samuel French, London, 1959. Another play which focuses on soldiers without a way of escape.

The Dumb Waiter, The Long and the Short and the Tall and *In Camera* are available in Penguin paperback editions.

R. P. Hewett: *A Choice of Dramatic Themes*, Harrap, London, 1973.

Unit 2

'O What is that Sound?'

Please read W. H. Auden's poem which is printed below. After a preliminary private reading listen to the poem read by a tutor or member of the group, concentrating particularly on the mounting tension and the dialogue of the two characters.

O what is that sound which so thrills the ear
  Down in the valley drumming, drumming?
Only the scarlet soldiers, dear,
  The soldiers coming.

O what is that light I see flashing so clear
  Over the distance brightly, brightly?
Only the sun on their weapons, dear,
  As they step lightly.

O what are they doing with all that gear,
  What are they doing this morning, this morning?
Only their usual manoeuvres, dear,
  Or perhaps a warning.

O why have they left the road down there,
  Why are they suddenly wheeling, wheeling?
Perhaps a change in their orders, dear.
  Why are you kneeling?

O haven't they stopped for the doctor's care,
  Haven't they reined their horses, their horses?
Why, they are none of them wounded, dear,
  None of these forces.

O is it the parson they want, with white hair,
　　Is it the parson, is it, is it?
No, they are passing his gateway, dear,
　　Without a visit.

O it must be the farmer who lives so near.
　　It must be the farmer so cunning, so cunning?
They have passed the farmyard already, dear,
　　And now they are running.

O where are you going? Stay with me here!
　　Were the vows you swore deceiving, deceiving?
No, but I promised to love you, dear,
　　But I must be leaving.

O it's broken the lock and splintered the door,
　　O it's the gate where they're turning, turning
Their boots are heavy on the floor
　　And their eyes are burning.

DISCUSSION AND ACTIVITY

1. In small groups discuss the possible reasons for the action of the soldiers and the attitude of the husband—or was he a husband?
2. Select a particular historical period in which the incidents

might have taken place; try to link the poem with an actual event.

3. Devise a short scene showing what happened beyond the end of the poem. The illustration to this unit may provide a starting-point.

4. Act out the poem itself; several possible approaches are suggested here but you should only use these if they are helpful:

(*a*) Use the dialogue of the poem and add sound effects to produce a short radio play which can be taped.

(*b*) Act the scene without speech while some of the group read the poem to the beat of a drum.

(*c*) Evolve a play which deals with similar events in any period of history.

(*d*) Select suitable music and show the scene in movement only.

Whatever you decide you will be aware of the need to make *specific* decisions; this is true of all work in drama: some of the questions you might need to answer are—how old are the characters? what is their relationship? where is the scene taking place? what are they wearing? You may wish to give some of the answers in written form or as diagrams and drawings.

5. Auden's short poem contains a matter of serious and deep concern. It is important not to allow your improvisations or playmaking on the poem to become superficial or frivolous. A central feature of drama is its ability to deal with complicated issues in straightforward human terms. You might discuss how this is achieved in a play that you see as a group.

BIBLIOGRAPHY

Baldwin & Whitehead (eds): *That Way and This*, Chatto & Windus, London, 1972. Poetry for creative drama and dance.

Alan Brownjohn (ed.): *First I Say This*, Hutchinson, London, 1969. Contains many poems which may repay similar experiments, e.g. John Gay's 'Fire in the City' and the section entitled 'Hear My Sad Story'.

Plate I

Plate II

Plate III

*Photographs
by courtesy of
Rank Strand Electrics*

Unit 3

The Stage

Study the illustrations of three contrasting theatres. Plays are performed on all these stages but probably Plate I comes nearest to your idea of a stage. What does the stage of your local theatre look like?

During recent years there have been many departures from the 'proscenium arch' type stage which had become firmly established at the beginning of the twentieth century. In Britain Stephen Joseph pioneered the 'theatre-in-the-round' in which the audience completely surround the acting space: the Library Theatre at Scarborough (Plate II) and the Victoria Theatre, Stoke-on-Trent are examples of his influence.

'Thrust' and 'apron' stages which project into the auditorium have gained in popularity. Modern theatres such as the Questors' Theatre (Plate III) can be adapted to several styles which allow maximum flexibility.

One of the most interesting of new theatres, the Churchill, is under construction in the London Borough of Bromley. This is a 'library theatre'—part of the trend to incorporate theatres in cultural centres. With a seating capacity of 750 it is estimated to have a final cost in excess of £1,000,000. Describing the project the Borough Architect Aneurin John writes:

'There is to be a high degree of mechanisation on the stage which you will see from the drawings has two rolling stages, each with a revolve in the wing space, and a set lift capable of transferring set trucks from the under-stage area. The whole of this machinery is designed to promote flexible use of the theatre and facilitate scene changing with the minimum manpower.'

DISCUSSION AND ACTIVITY

1. Examine the drawings of the Churchill Theatre on pages 27, 28 and use the glossary to help you in establishing the details of Aneurin John's description.

2. Look at illustrations of the Greek and Elizabethan theatres and see if you can identify similar features in modern theatre buildings.

3. If possible, try out some of your work from Unit 2 in the round, on a thrust stage shape and on a proscenium stage. What problems arise in each case?

4. Make a collection of sketches or photographs illustrating as many different kinds of stages as possible. The books listed in the bibliography section will help your research.

5. Arrange a visit to a local theatre and find the stage dimensions. Notice any mechanism for raising sections of the floor and where the lighting controls are sited.

During the City of London Festival, 1972, a London bus was used as a 'street theatre': try to discover any other types of unusual staging currently being employed.

section 'dd'

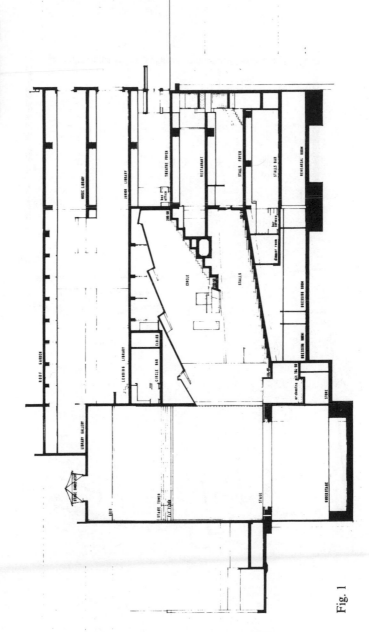

ROOF GARDEN

LIBRARY GALLERY

MUSIC LIBRARY

JUNIOR LIBRARY

LENDING LIBRARY

CLUBS

CIRCLE BAR

STORE SHADOWS

GRID

STAGE TOWER

THEATRE FOYER

RESTAURANT

box office

CIRCLE

STALLS

STALLS FOYER

STALLS BAR

REHEARSAL ROOM

dressing room

DRESSING ROOM

DRESSING ROOM

or-chestra

STORE

STAGE

UNDERSTAGE

Fig. 1

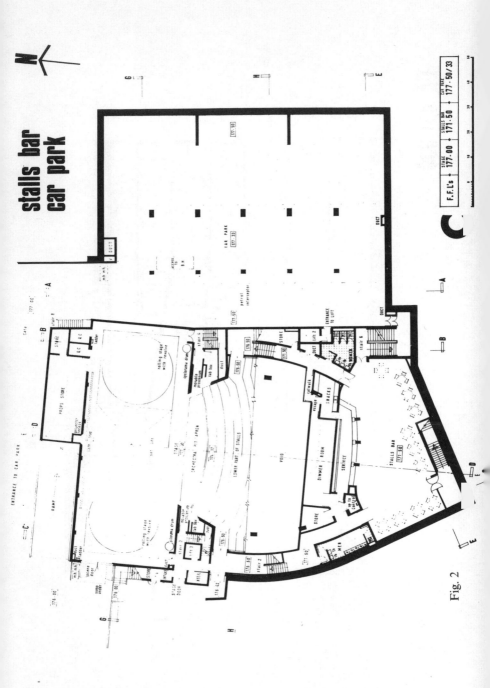

stalls bar
car park

Fig. 2

BIBLIOGRAPHY

David Adland: *Group Approach to Drama 6*, Longmans, London, 1972.
    The section entitled 'Theatre' examines many of the ideas relevant to
    this Unit.
Frederick Bentham: *New Theatres in Britain*, Rank-Strand, London, 1970.
Peter Brook: *The Empty Space*, Pelican, Harmondsworth, 1972.
Phyllis Hartnoll: *A Concise History of the Theatre*, Thames & Hudson,
    London, 1968.
Stephen Joseph: *Theatre in the Round*, Pitman, London, 1955.
David Male: *The Story of the Theatre*, A. & C. Black, London, 1967.
J. B. Priestley: *The Wonderful World of the Theatre*, Macdonald, London,
    1969.
Richard Southern: *The Seven Ages of the Theatre*, Faber, London, 1968.
Simon Tidworth: *Theatres—an Illustrated History*, Pall Mall, London,
    1973.

Unit 4

Some Consequences

Recent innovations in theatre design have given rise to a greater sense of intimacy between actors and audience. As in the Elizabethan theatre, actors can now see more of their audience and the audience are in much closer proximity to the actor. Many directors feel these developments to be extremely valuable and, in large theatres, actors sometimes make excursions into the audience in an attempt to involve them in a more vital way.

Towards the end of the nineteenth century, the proscenium arch was regarded as a fourth wall. This was taken to an extreme by the French director, André Antoine (1858–1943) who actually had a temporary 'wall' built across the proscenium for rehearsals and then removed it for the first performance. This idea still survives.

If you read the opening speech of Shakespeare's *Henry V*, you will find that the Chorus speaks directly to the audience inviting them to use their imagination as they watch the performance. Puck's closing speech of *A Midsummer Night's Dream* invites the audience to applaud if they have enjoyed the play. Direct speech to the audience is not an entirely new idea.

Now look at the following speeches from three twentieth-century plays.

From: *A Man for all Seasons* by Robert Bolt.

ACT ONE

(When the curtain rises, the set is in darkness but for a single spot which descends vertically upon the COMMON MAN, *who stands in front of a big property basket.)*

COMMON MAN: It is perverse! To start a play made up of Kings and Cardinals in speaking costumes and intellectuals with embroidered mouths, with me.

If a King or a Cardinal had done the prologue he'd have had the right materials. And an intellectual would have shown enough majestic meanings, coloured propositions, and closely woven liturgical stuff to dress the House of Lords! But this!

Is this a costume? Does this say anything? It barely covers one man's nakedness! A bit of black material to reduce Old Adam to the Common Man.

Oh, if they'd let me come on naked, I could have shown you something of my own. Which would have told you without words—! . . . Something I've forgotten . . . Old Adam's muffled up.

(Backing towards basket.) Well, for a proposition of my own, I need a costume. *(Takes out and puts on the coat and hat of* STEWARD.)

Matthew! The Household Steward of Sir Thomas More! *(Lights come up swiftly on set. He takes from the basket five silver goblets, one larger than the others, and a jug with a lid, with which he furnishes the table. A burst of conversational merriment off; he pauses and indicates head of stairs.)* There's company to dinner. *(Finishes business at table.)*

All right! A Common Man! A sixteenth-century Butler! *(He drinks from the jug.)* All right—the six—*(Breaks off, agreeably surprised by the quality of the liquor, regards the jug respectfully, and drinks again.)* The sixteenth century is the Century of the Common Man. *(Puts down the jug.)* Like all the other centuries. *(Crossing right.)* And that's my proposition.

From: *Murder in the Cathedral* by T. S. Eliot.

INTERLUDE

THE ARCHBISHOP
preaches in the Cathedral on Christmas Morning, 1170

'Glory to God in the highest,[1] and on earth peace to men of good will.' *The fourteenth verse of the second chapter of the Gospel according to Saint Luke.* In the Name of the Father, and of the Son, and of the Holy Ghost. Amen.

Dear children of God, my sermon this Christmas morning will be a very short one. I wish only that you should meditate in your hearts the deep meaning and mystery of our masses of Christmas Day. For whenever Mass is said, we re-enact the Passion and Death of Our Lord; and on this Christmas Day we do this in celebration of His Birth. So that at the same moment we rejoice in His coming for the salvation of men, and offer again to God His Body and Blood in sacrifice, oblation and satisfaction for the sins of the whole world. It was in this same night that has just passed, that a multitude of the heavenly host appeared before the shepherds at Bethlehem, saying 'Glory to God in the highest, and on earth peace to men of good will'; at this same time of all the year that we celebrate at once the Birth of Our Lord and His Passion and Death upon the Cross. Beloved, as the World sees, this is to behave in a strange fashion. For who in the World will both mourn and rejoice at once and for the same reason? For either joy will be overborne by mourning, or mourning will be cast out by joy; so it is only in these our Christian mysteries that we can rejoice and mourn at once for the same reason. Now think for a moment about the meaning of this word 'peace'. Does it seem strange to you that the angels should have announced Peace, when ceaselessly the world has been stricken with War and the fear of War? Does it seem to you that the angelic voices were mistaken, and that the promise was a disappointment and a cheat?

Reflect now, how Our Lord Himself spoke of Peace. He said to His disciples, 'Peace I leave with you, my peace I give unto you.'[2] Did He mean peace as we think of it: the kingdom of England at peace with its neighbours, the barons at peace with the King, the householder counting over his peaceful gains, the swept hearth, his best wine for a friend at the table, his wife singing to the children? Those men His disciples knew no such things: they went forth to journey afar, to suffer by land and sea, to know torture, imprisonment, disappointment, to suffer death by martyrdom. What then did He mean? If you ask that, remember then that He said also, 'Not as the world gives, give I unto you.'

So then, He gave to His disciples peace, but not peace as the world gives.

Consider also one thing of which you have probably never thought. Not only do we at the feast of Christmas celebrate at once Our Lord's Birth and His Death: but on the next day we celebrate the martyrdom of His first martyr, the blessed Stephen. Is it an accident, do you think, that the day of the first martyr follows immediately the day of the Birth of Christ? By no means. Just as we rejoice and mourn at once, in the Birth and in the Passion of Our Lord; so also, in a smaller figure, we both rejoice and mourn in the death of martyrs. We mourn, for the sins of the world that has martyred them; we rejoice, that another soul is numbered among the Saints in Heaven, for the glory of God and for the salvation of men.

Beloved, we do not think of a martyr simply as a good Christian who has been killed because he is a Christian: for that would be solely to mourn. We do not think of him simply as a good Christian who has been elevated to the company of the Saints: for that would be simply to rejoice: and neither our mourning nor our rejoicing is as the world's is. A Christian martyrdom is never an accident, for Saints are not made by accident. Still less is a Christian martyrdom the effect of a man's will to become a Saint, as a man by willing and contriving may become a ruler of men. A martyrdom is always the design of God, for His love of men, to warn them and to lead them, to bring them back to His ways. It is never the design of man; for the true martyr is he who has become the instrument of God, who has lost his will in the will of God,³ and who no longer desires anything for himself, not even the glory of being a martyr. So thus as on earth the Church mourns and rejoices at once, in a fashion that the world cannot understand; so in Heaven the Saints are most high, having made themselves most low, and are seen, not as we see them, but in the light of the Godhead from which they draw their being.

I have spoken to you to-day, dear children of God, of the martyrs of the past, asking you to remember especially our martyr of Canterbury, the blessed Archbishop Elphege; because it is fitting, on Christ's birthday, to remember what is that Peace which He brought; and because, dear children, I do not think I shall ever preach to you again; and because it is possible that in a short time you may have yet another martyr, and that one perhaps not the last. I would have you keep in your hearts these words that I say, and think of them at another time. In the Name of the Father, and of the Son, and of the Holy Ghost. Amen.

From: *Luther* by John Osborne.

ACT TWO

SCENE ONE

The market place, Juterbög, 1517. The sound of loud music, bells as a procession approaches the centre of the market place, which is covered in the banners of welcoming trade guilds. At the head of the slow-moving procession, with its lighted tapers and to the accompaniment of singing, prayers and the smoke of incense, is carried the Pontiff's bull of grace on a cushion and cloth of gold. Behind this the arms of the Pope and the Medici. After this, carrying a large red wooden cross, comes the focus of the procession, JOHN TETZEL, *Dominican, inquisitor and most famed and successful indulgence vendor of his day. He is splendidly equipped to be an ecclesiastical huckster, with alive, silver hair, the powerfully calculating voice, range and technique of a trained orator, the terrible, riveting charm of a dedicated professional able to winkle coppers out of the pockets of the poor and desperate.*

The red cross is taken from TETZEL *and established prominently behind him, and, from it are suspended the arms of the Pope.*

TETZEL: Are you wondering who I am, or what I am? Is there anyone here among you, any small child, any cripple, or any sick idiot who hasn't heard of me, and doesn't know why I am here? No? No? Well, speak up then if there is? What, no one? Do you all know me then? Do you all know who I am? If it's true, it's very good, and just as it should be. Just as it should be, and no more than that! However, however—just in case—just in case, mind, there is one blind, maimed midget among you today who can't hear, I will open his ears and wash them out with sacred soap for him! And, as for the rest of you. I know I can rely on you all to listen patiently while I instruct him. Is that right? Can I go on? I'm asking you, is that right, can I go on? I say 'can I go on'?
(Pause)
Thank you. And what is there to tell this blind, maimed midget who's down there somewhere among you? No, don't look round for him, you'll

only scare him and then he'll lose his one great
chance, and it's not likely to come again, or if it
does come, maybe it'll be too late. Well, what's the
good news on this bright day? What's the information
you want? It's this! Who is this friar with his red
cross? Who sent him, and what's he here for?
Don't try to work it out for yourself because I'm
going to tell you now, this very minute. I am John
Tetzel, Dominican, inquisitor, sub-commissioner to
the Archbishop of Mainz, and what I bring you is
indulgences. Indulgences made possible by the red
blood of Jesus Christ, and the red cross you see
standing up here behind me is the standard of those
who carry them. Look at it! Go on, look at it!
What else do you see hanging from the red cross?
Well, what do they look like? Why, it's the arms of
his holiness, because why? Because it's him who sent
me here. Yes, my friend, the Pope himself has sent
me with indulgences for you! Fine, you say, but
what are indulgences? And what are they to me?
What are indulgences? They're only the most
precious and noble of God's gifts to men, that's all
they are! Before God, I tell you I wouldn't swap my
privilege at this moment with that of St. Peter in
Heaven because I've already saved more souls with
my indulgences than he could ever have done with
all his sermons. You think that's bragging, do you?
Well, listen a little more carefully, my friend,
because this concerns *you*! Just look at it this way.
For every mortal sin you commit, the Church says
that after confession and contrition, you've got to do
penance—either in this life or in purgatory—for
seven years. Seven years! Right? Are you with me?
Good. Now then, how many mortal sins are
committed by you—by you—in a single day? Just
think for one moment: in one single day of your life.
Do you know the answer? Oh, not so much as one
a day. Very well then, how many in a month? How
many in six months? How many in a year? And
how many in a whole lifetime? Yes, you needn't
shuffle your feet—it doesn't bear thinking about
does it? You couldn't even add up all those years
without a merchant's clerk to do it for you! Try
and add up all the years of torment piling up! What

about it? And isn't there anything you can do about
this terrible situation you're in? Do you really want
to know? Yes! There is something, and that
something I have here with me now up here, letters,
letters of indulgence. Hold up the letters so that
everyone can see them. Is there anyone so small he
can't see? Look at them, all properly sealed, an
indulgence in every envelope, and one of them can
be yours today, now, before it's too late! Come on,
come up as close as you like, you won't squash me
so easily. Take a good look. There isn't any one sin so
big that one of these letters can't remit it. I challenge
any one here, any member of this audience, to
present me with a sin, anything, any kind of a sin, I
don't care what it is, that I can't settle for him with
one of these precious little envelopes. Why, if any
one had ever offered violence to the blessed Virgin
Mary, Mother of God, if he'd only pay up—as long
as he paid up all he could—he'd find himself
forgiven. You think I'm exaggerating? You do, do
you? Well, I'm authorized to go even further than
that. Not only am I empowered to give you these
letters of pardon for the sins you've already
committed, I can give you pardon for those sins you
haven't even committed (*pause . . . then slowly*) but,
which, however you *intend* to commit! But, you ask
—and it's a fair question—but, you ask, why is our
Holy Lord prepared to distribute such a rich grace
to me? The answer, my friends, is all too simple.
It's so that we can restore the ruined church of St.
Peter and St. Paul in Rome! So that it won't have
its equal anywhere in the world. This great church
contains the bodies not only of the holy apostles
Peter and Paul, but of a hundred thousand martyrs
and no less than forty-six popes! To say nothing of
the relics like St. Veronica's handkerchief, the
burning bush of Moses and the very rope with
which Judas Iscariot hanged himself! But, alas, this
fine old building is threatened with destruction, and
all these things with it, if a sufficient restoration fund
isn't raised, and raised soon. (*With passionate irony*)
. . . Will anyone dare to say that the cause is not a
good one? (*Pause.*) . . . Very well, and won't you,
for as little as one quarter of a florin, my friend,

buy yourself one of these letters, so that in the hour
of death, the gate through which sinners enter the
world of torment shall be closed against you, and
the gate leading to the joy of paradise be flung open
for you? And, remember this, these letters aren't
just for the living but for the dead too. There can't
be one amongst you who hasn't at least one dear
one who has departed—and to who knows what?
Why, these letters are for them too. It isn't even
necessary to repent. So don't hold back, come
forward, think of your dear ones, think of
yourselves! For twelve groats, or whatever it is we
think you can afford, you can rescue your father
from agony and yourself from certain disaster. And
if you only have the coat on your back to call your
own, then strip it off, strip it off now so that you
too can obtain grace. For remember: As soon as
your money rattles in the box and the cash bell
rings, the soul flies out of purgatory and sings! So,
come on then. Get your money out! What is it then,
have your wits flown away with your faith? Listen
then, soon, I shall take down the cross, shut the
gates of heaven, and put out the brightness of this
sun of grace that shines on you here today.
(*He flings a large coin into the open strong box, where
it rattles furiously.*)
The Lord our God reigns no longer. He has
resigned all power to the Pope. In the name of the
Father, and of the Son and of the Holy Ghost.
Amen.
(*The sound of coins clattering like rain into a great
coffer as the light fades.*)

DISCUSSION AND ACTIVITY

1. In all three speeches the playwright has adopted the
style of direct address to the audience. In *Murder in the
Cathedral*, Becket's speech is in the form of a sermon which
divides the two halves of the play. Temporarily the audience
become the congregation whom the Archbishop addresses.
(Later in the play the audience are involved in very different
terms. Look at the Knights' closing speeches.) In *Luther* the
speaker, Tetzel, is a brilliant orator, apparently speaking

to the crowd on the stage, but in performance he seems to include the audience as well. The Common Man, in Robert Bolt's play, is alone on the stage lit only by a spotlight. What do you think the author's intention is in using that opening? He is certainly breaking through the 'fourth wall' straight away. Does this speech have anything in common with the Chorus who starts *Henry V*?

When you go to a theatrical performance, whether it is a school play, a local dramatic society, a repertory company or a large professional group, notice how the actors use the stage. Do they use entrances through the auditorium? Does the play include any speeches directed straight to the audience? How do these approaches affect your enjoyment and understanding of the play? Another play by John Osborne called *The Entertainer* includes short interludes by a music hall comic. You might like to read any of these extracts and devise ways in which you would stage them. The plans in Unit 3 give examples of some of the choices available. Remember to indicate where the audience will be sitting.

If it is difficult to visit the theatre, watch how the producers of television programmes involve the audience. *Top of the Pops* and *Top of the Form*, quizzes and light comedy shows include shots of the audience. In some cases the laughter of an unseen audience is heard. What effect does this have on your view of the programme?

2. At the height of his powers the great actor Henry Irving visited Canterbury and in the cathedral chapter house he held an audience spellbound for three hours while he read from Tennyson's play *Becket*.

Try out the speeches in this Unit with your group as audience after making suggestions for suitable staging.

3. Evolve an improvisation entitled 'You're Next' which quite literally involves the audience and then discuss its effectiveness with them.

4. In David Campton's play *In Committee* (Unit 12) the idea of audience participation becomes a marked feature— but does physical involvement necessarily mean a richer theatrical experience?

Unit 5

Improvisation

You are probably familiar with the word 'improvise' in the sense of 'making do', using anything handy to mend an engine or piece of apparatus that has broken down. The repair is not always very efficient but it is temporarily satisfactory. In drama the word has a very different meaning. Improvisation in drama is acting which does not directly arise from a script; it forms one of the most important elements in the training of an actor or actress today.

In working out the suggestion in Units 1–4 you have probably employed improvisation techniques without realising it. There is nothing second-rate, temporary or superficial about improvisation in drama. It is serious, thought-provoking and demanding for the participants when it is properly experienced. This is a very simplified description. The books listed at the end of the unit, particularly Hodgson and Richards' *Improvisation* or Pickering's *Drama Improvised* give very full accounts of this aspect of drama.

In the late nineteenth century the great Russian director Stanislavsky (1863–1938) laid the foundations of what we now understand as improvisation. His system of training for actors depended on establishing the truthful portrayal of their action. A deep understanding of the psychology of the character and his particular motives was essential. His thoughts, actions, desires and attitudes had to be discovered. Actors were encouraged to consider how the character they were studying would behave in situations other than those shown in the play. Great concentration and sincerity were required.

These ideas were in direct contrast to the artificial and

contrived acting of that period. Stanislavsky had a close association with the most famous of Russian playwrights, Chekhov. The Moscow Arts Theatre where Chekhov's plays were performed became a shrine of 'absolute realism'. Though the two men frequently argued, the effect of their combined skills was to emphasise the 'reality' of drama, i.e. believing that the characters portrayed were not romantic, escapist figures existing only in the theatre, but human beings, suffering, facing problems or experiencing the joys of real life.

More recently some theatre performances have taken place which have never involved the use of a script but have depended entirely on the improvisational skills of the actors. To some extent this reflects the influence of music hall techniques. The audience are constantly on tenterhooks because neither they nor the cast know what to expect.

Pantomime, some ballet characters and Punch and Judy are the remnants of an old form of improvisational drama known as the *Commedia dell' Arte* which developed in Italy in the sixteenth century. Whilst there was some kind of script called the 'scenario', the performers had to fill out the actions and dialogue by their own efforts. Some of the important characters were Pantalone, a rather short-sighted, greedy father, Dottore, a self-important teacher or physician, Capitano, a boasting soldier and Arlecchino (Harlequin), a cheeky servant. The situations were usually comic, involving a good deal of knockabout comedy.

DISCUSSION AND ACTIVITY

1. Look at the pictures from a textbook on acting published in 1897. The chapter entitled 'The Head, Face, Eyes, Brows and Mouth' gives careful instructions as to how actors and actresses can achieve the appearance of various emotions by a variety of facial expressions and head positions.

The Head—The head must be held in an erect and natural position, its movements must be suited to the character and delivery, accord with the gestures, and harmonise with the hands and motions of the body.

a Hatred

b Rage

c Fear

The *according* actions of the head and hand are—when the hand seeks the head, the head bends forward to meet it; when the hand moves from the head, the head is held back or averted; in submission, when the hands are prone, it bends downward. The head, without the aid of the expressive face, performs many useful and appropriate expressions.

When hung down, humility, shame, and grief are expressed.

When turned up, arrogance, pride, and courage are shown.

When inclined to one side, languor, mental derangement.

When stiff, rigid, and thrust forward, nobility, barbarity, brutality; all other positions indicating modesty, doubt, admiration, indignation.

A Nod . . . Signifies assent, willingness, or approbation.

A Shake . . . Signifies disapprobation, annoyance, and rejection.

A Toss . . . Contempt, indignation.
Averted . . . In dislike or horror.
Forward . . . In attention, interest, apprehension.
And besides these, impressions created by position nearly all belong to significant gestures.

The Face—The face is, of course, the sublime fountain of complete convincing, perfect expression, and in order to accomplish the various motions we must consider the different parts separately, but the eye, eyelids, and eyebrows may be taken together under the heading of:

The Eye—'They burn, they strain, they twinkle, they swim; they are savage, fierce, flaming, and serious, distorted, submissive, insinuating, and sensual', and yet this wonderful assemblage is composed simply of circles of various colours, which indicate the direction from, or to which, impressions tend.

Practise moving the eyeball in all directions slowly whilst the eyelids are raised and steady. The eye proper requires the operation of the lids to create perfect expressions.

There is a difference between the eye of a man and the eye of a woman. The former possesses the epic, philosophical, and intellectual; the latter is formed for its softness and brilliancy, for the exercise of tender sentiments, characteristic delicacy, vitality, intelligence, and truth.

Women frequently destroy the distinguishing characteristics of their eyes by a thick line of paint on the under lid. This is an error; the upper lid is the striking feature upon which much of the character depends and might be strongly marked; the lower lash does not in any degree contribute to the marking of the eye, and should be kept light and tender to softly merge into the cheek.

Form and expression depend, as I have said, on the eyelids and position of the head, and intensity is strongly marked by the eyebrows. The eyes are the 'index of the mind,' the

> Strong-felt passion bolts into the face—
> The mind untouch'd, what is it but grimace?

The muscles of the eyes obey the will, and also act

involuntarily, subject to the affections of the mind. Their complicated fibres serve no purpose but to convey impressions to the soul, and to give external expression to them. 'We touch each other by the sense of sight,' and the *eyebrow* plays an important part, giving the form to the eye in different degrees, and governing the forehead, more peculiarly in man than in woman. Its elevation is indicative of intellectual power; it is arched in doubt, surprise, or fear, laughter and admiration; contracted towards the nose, and lowered in rage, despair, jealousy; and in grief and pain contracted and raised upwards towards the inner extremities. They can move together or separately in the different sentiments they wish to convey.

The Nose—The nose seldom manifests our feelings, in spite of the fact that derision, contempt, pride, and power are conveyed by it. It is inelegant to inflate and move the nostrils, to disturb them by forcing the breath through with violence, to put your fingers to them. Let the nose alone, as nature formed it, long or short, thick or thin, flat or *retroussé*, Grecian, Roman or composite. The French say, 'Le nez n'a jamais gâté beauté.' The nose of itself expresses a vast deal, and, like the cheeks and chin, is incapable of much cultivation.

For 'make-up' purposes we may remember that full, clear, fleshy cheeks indicate sensitiveness, generosity, nobleness, mildness, sensuality.

Thin and *shrunk*, not addicted to life's enjoyment—hard, rigid, unsympathetic.

Hollow, grief, pain.

A Projecting Chin . . . Signifies a positive mind.

A Retreating Chin . . . Weakness and deficiency.

A Sharp Chin . . . Acuteness and craft.

A Double Chin . . . Indolence, sensuality.

Angular Chins . . . Belong to the discreet, firm, well-disposed.

Flat Chins . . . Cold and dry temperament.

Small Chins . . . Timidity.

Round Chins with Dimple . . . Kindness.

Sharp indentations in the middle of the chin to suggest a judicious, calm understanding, resolute perception.

The Mouth—We are often asked, 'Which is the most expressive feature, the mouth or the eyes? Without detracting in the least degree from the exquisite functions of the eyes, we think we must fairly say the lips, the seat of smiles and amiability, grace, and sweetness, 'where composure calms, discretion keeps the door.' The mouth is the 'vestibule of the soul, the door of eloquence'. Every bad habit defaces its soft beauty, and leaves injurious traces. Intemperance discolours and distorts it; ill-nature wrinkles it, envy and malice deform it; voluptuousness bloats it; ill-health and sorrow affect it perceptibly. We look to the mouth for its perfect articulations, which delight the eye as well as the ear.

The lower lip is the active organ; the opening of the mouth puts all the other organs in a stage of readiness for effort.

Compressed . . . It indicates decision of character, resolution of purpose.

Open . . . Vacancy, idiocy.

For Mirth . . . The angles are drawn upwards and backwards, exposing the teeth, and violently opened also for contempt or fear.

For Rage . . . Downwards and backwards, unevenly showing canine teeth; the same in different degrees for peevishness, discontent, jealousy, and fear.

For Devotion . . . Lips slightly parted.

By Henry Neville, Actor and Dramatist.

You can understand why Stanislavsky was so dissatisfied with the grimacing, gesturing actors who applied those mechanical techniques.

2. Devise a series of *ideas* that give an opportunity for the emotions of hatred, fear and rage to be expressed without using the 'theatrical' expressions pictured in the acting textbook.

3. Find out some real-life situations reported in the newspaper or described in a book, poem or play which involve the emotions you have investigated. They may provide the basis for some experiments in improvisation.

4. Read chapters 3 (section II) and 11 of Stanislavsky's *An*

Actor Prepares and notice the discipline he imposed on his students.

5. Stanislavsky once wrote: 'an actor can hold the attention of an audience by himself in a highly dramatic scene for at most seven minutes (that is the absolute maximum!). In a quiet scene the maximum is one minute (this, too, is a lot!). After that the diversity of the actor's means of expression is not sufficient to hold the attention of the audience, and he is forced to repeat himself with the result that the attention of the audience slackens until the next climax which requires new methods of presentation. But please, note that this is only true in the case of geniuses.'

How does this apply to your experience of the speeches in Unit 4?

6. Look up the *Commedia dell' Arte* and acquaint yourself with some of the stock characters and plots. Is there evidence in any of Shakespeare's plays of the influence of the *Commedia*? e.g. Sir Toby Belch and Feste in *Twelfth Night* and Trinculo and Stephano in *The Tempest*.

7. Devise a group improvisation called 'Gas' and ensure *absolute* concentration throughout. The theme may be serious, e.g. 'Poison Gas', or comic, e.g. 'Laughing Gas'.

8. Improvisation includes inventing appropriate speech for the situation. This is often a difficulty. It is useful to decide whether you are inventing speech for *yourself* in a particular situation or creating a separate character whose speech is different from your own. Try to write down or record snatches of conversations or speeches that seem to exemplify particular characters. You will have to work on your vocal dexterity to handle the language effectively. It takes a good deal of concentration. Improvised interviews involving pop stars, sports personalities, foreign visitors, politicians, lawyers etc. will require different styles of speaking.

9. Do you use the same style of speaking in every situation in real life? Notice how your speech varies as you speak to: a friend, an employer, a shop assistant, parents, a younger brother or sister. An equal variety should be noticeable in your vocal improvisations.

10. What are the advantages and disadvantages of improvised speech in a performance?

BIBLIOGRAPHY

For a consideration of improvisation in school, college and theatre:
John Hodgson and Ernest Richards: *Improvisation*, Methuen, London, 1966.
David Male: *Approaches to Drama*, Allen & Unwin, London, 1973.
For quick ideas for simple and extended improvisations:
Robert Newton: *Exercise Improvisation*, J. Garnet Miller, London, 1960.
Kenneth Pickering: *Drama Improvised*, J. Garnet Miller, London, 1971.
For reference:
Giacomo Oreglia: *The Commedia dell' Arte*, Methuen, London, 1968.
Pierre Louis Duchartre: *The Italian Comedy*, Dover, London & New York, 1929.
Acting in the Sixties, BBC, London, 1970.
Phyllis Hartnoll: *Oxford Companion to the Theatre*, OUP, London, 1967.
K. Stanislavsky: *An Actor Prepares*, Penguin, Harmondsworth.

Unit 6

'Uneasy Lies the Head'

The visual impact of a play is an important part of the performance. 'Dressing up' was quite probably one of your first dramatic experiences. You may recall when as a child, that draping a simple piece of cloth over your shoulders transformed you into a king, a witch or a ghost. A box became a boat, the clothes-horse, a castle.

The following article dealing with the popular TV series *Elizabeth R* gives some insight into the problems that arise when accuracy and effect are of equal importance.

> To be a king and wear a crown is a thing more glorious to them that see it than pleasant to them that bear it.
>
> Elizabeth, in her last speech to Parliament

To achieve Elizabeth's severe and remote style of beauty, Glenda Jackson has shaved her hair back to the crown so that her forehead can fall clear from her rear set wig. She wears an artificial, straight nose which grows thinner and bonier as the years pass, and the Elizabethan accomplishments she has had to master include writing in italic script, riding side-saddle, playing the virginals and dancing the Galliard, La Volta and the Pavane. Her make-up takes account of the smallpox that scarred the Queen in the 1560s.

When Elizabeth died she left 2,000 dresses, many of them immortalised by contemporary portraits, and these form the basis of the costumes made for the six plays.

In fact, fashion historians should be able to look at every costume Glenda Jackson wears and link it with a surviving portrait of the Queen.

Elizabeth's garments became more and more fantastic as she grew older and tried to hide her age inside elaborate confections of lace and jewels. Indeed one fascinating discovery made by the researchers of *Elizabeth R* is that some of these later costumes are actually impossible to make: artists anxious to represent visually the Queen's idea of her own magnificence painted halo-like veils and ruffs that cannot possibly be supported by modern artificial strengtheners, let alone by creations of 16th-century lace and bone.

'Of course it's very easy to get bogged down in the historical details' says producer Roderick Graham. 'And there's a terrible temptation to put in lines like "The new play at the Globe by a talented lad just come to town from Stratford. He should go far." But I hope we've avoided the commonplaces of costume drama.'

Under powerful artificial lighting and at a distance, normal dressmaking materials are of little use. Stage costumes demand heavier textured fabrics and bolder designs if they are not to appear flat and uninteresting. Fabrics such as hessian (rather like sacking) or worn velvet curtaining trimmed with painted or sprayed rope can create an appearance of amazing richness when made up into costumes. Their broken surface reflects the light and deepens the shadow. Many plain fabrics need texturing—sometimes with powder colour applied with a rag-covered paint roller; sometimes sprayed on and even in the form of dry leaves glued to the surface.

Costumes, armour and jewellery all present considerable

problems: three articles containing many helpful suggestions appeared in the magazine *Vox* in 1972—they are reproduced here.

ARMOUR: DOUGLAS WALTERS

MAKING A GREEK HELMET

Technique in the use of plastic emulsion
Any of the following is suitable:
Emulsion Glaze, Brodie & Middleton Ltd, 79 Long Acre, London, W.C.2.
Reeves' Polymer Varnish
Marvin Medium, Margros, Monument House, Woking, Surrey.

These plastic emulsions dry quickly and are excellent for layers of pasted papier mâché. Card wood and rope may be securely bonded with them.

If you are not satisfied with the form of the object you are making, it is possible to perform a kind of plastic surgery with a sharp knife. Pieces may be cut out of your model and others inserted, glued and layered with tissue and emulsion. This work is really a kind of sculpture. Inspiration may be found in books on paper sculpture.

Making the helmet
The problem is that of making a helmet which is basically a kind of half-egg shape, from a flat sheet of card. On to this other forms are added. The fitting is very important and it is better to err on the large side and fill it out with foam rubber than make it too small.

Figure 3 shows two different views of the helmet that is to be made, as well as drawings showing its separate parts and their construction. Below, on the right, is the pattern from which the parts are constructed.

The crest
Make a template for the crest in stiff paper. Experiment until you get a shape that pleases you and then cut out two similar shapes in thick card. To make it straight and rigid, the crest should be given a thickness. This may be done by using balsa wood, expanded polystyrene, match or toothpaste boxes or any other similar light-weight material. Cut out strips of card with little triangular tabs along the length and glue them along the thickness of the crest.

The half-egg shape

The flat pattern for this is given in the bottom right-hand corner of the illustration. This is a sheet of card, not too thick, $12\frac{1}{4}$ in. × $12\frac{1}{4}$ in. The black lines are to be cut through. This makes 26 strips, 13 on each side of the central spine, which is to go over the head from front to back. The central spine is 1 in. wide and from the middle strip extends 5 in. on each side.

The ends of the strips A, B, C, and D, E, F are gathered together and glued so that the two outer strips butt end to end and overlap the middle strip. This makes a construction that will already fit the head.

Now the remaining strips are to be arranged so as to form the dome-shape that fits on to the skull. They are to be gathered rather in the manner of a fan or a hand of cards. Take strip F and pull its adjacent strips together so that they are behind and pressing up and out towards it. Working outwards, repeat this process with the remaining strips and hold them in place with Sellotape. It does not matter how untidy the model looks at this stage. The object is to create a shapely, symmetrical form. View it from all angles. Now, having made the crest and the dome-shape, glue them together with impact adhesive.

The brow, cheek and neck pieces

These must be cut out of stiff paper and Sellotaped into place until an accurate fit and a good design are achieved. Cut them out of thick card and glue into place.

Finishing

It remains to give the helmet an appearance of weight and substance. Where you can see the thin edge of the card, make it appear thick by gluing rope to it. The thickness used for skipping rope is suitable. Using plastic emulsion, paste strips of tissue across the rope and down on to both sides of the card to bond both rope and card firmly. In doing this it is important to see that there are no air bubbles beneath the tissue paper, which should be firmly smoothed down with a stiff bristle brush. It is as well to cover the entire helmet with at least one layer of this type of papier mâché, inside and out. For the inside, use coloured paper. The outside will be painted but paint is not advisable where the helmet makes contact with the actor's head.

Decoration

This will be mainly on the crest, the brow and cheek pieces. It may take the form of a painted pattern or raised decoration. Relief may be made by modelled plasticene covered with papier mâché, pieces of lino block suitably cut and engraved, string, shaped metal foil, or even wine gums. The last two items may be used to represent jewels. The more relief you can create, the richer and more substantial the finished object will appear since whatever projects from the surface of the helmet not only reflects a highlight but is underlined by a shadow.

Painting

The choice of colour will be determined by the production with which you are concerned. Whatever you decide, a basic colour to cover the entire helmet is useful as it is then easier to see where decoration or relief is needed. The paint may be ordinary school powder colours or scene-painter's colours. Mix them with water

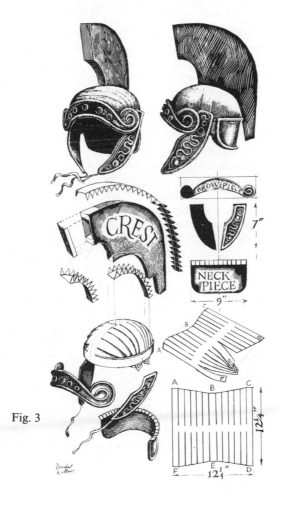

Fig. 3

to a thin cream and then add plastic emulsion. To create the effect of a bronze helmet, use a basic layer of some brownish colour—raw or burnt umber—and paint all the under surfaces with black as a false shadow. Taking a small amount of bronze metallic paint on the end of a stiff brush, work the paint out on newspaper and then drag the dry paint over the projecting surfaces of the helmet. Let the paint be thickest on the top and projecting surfaces; the hollows will remain untouched. The richest effect is always produced by broken colour. If silver is to be the metallic paint, use black as an underpainting.

STAGE JEWELLERY: CATHY HAINES

The design and making of stage jewellery cannot, of course, be seen as something separate from costume design generally; yet when a production gets under way and attention is focused on the design of costumes, it too often happens that the care lavished on these is not extended to the accessories although it is these very details that do so much to make or mar the overall effect. Only too frequently are the accessories—belts, bracelets, necklaces or brooches—rummaged from somebody's trinket box. People do not realise that ordinary jewellery is usually much too small and can look insignificant under stage lighting.

The basic rules for costume design apply no less to these small complementary items. The stage is always extremely deceptive: the most costly and magnificent brocade may lose its quality once it is seen under stage lights; even cloth of gold may look drab and dark, whereas gilded rubber can give an impression of untold wealth. The important thing is to find what inexpensive materials, with the help of imaginative treatment and paint, will give the best results. But before we pass to methods and materials, I must mention sources of ideas: these can be found in books containing reproductions of paintings, books on costumes, antique guides, well illustrated historical encyclopedias, etc.

When we have once decided on the pieces to be simulated, we should draw them on paper to the required size, remembering that stage jewellery needs to be bigger than jewellery in normal use. Once the designs are ready, we should begin to collect the materials needed.

I suggest a raid on the junk shops for broken necklaces and odd earrings, and the collection of screw-top lids from jam jars and sauce jars, odd bits of string and twine, curtain rings, and wire of any thickness. We shall also need plasticene, net or tarlatan, newspaper, polycell, odd strips of elastic, safety pins, Evostick, odd pieces of firm material, and gold, bronze and silver paints.

Most of the jewellery required will be rings or brooches and so I will outline some methods of making these. One way is to mould the basic shape required in plasticene. Then place over the top and side (but not the back) a layer of net or tarlatan, well soaked in polycell paste. Add layers of newspaper soaked in polycell and placed on in small strips, making sure to cover the whole area evenly. While the substance is still wet, make indentations where the stones are to be set, or make balls of paper and stick these on the required places and then cover with a few more layers of pasted paper. Let all this thoroughly dry.

The next stage is to glue on any further trimmings needed; string or twine, for example, when painted will give the effect of gold or silver wire. (I have found bronze paint highlighted in gold the most effective.) When the paint is dry, glue on the stones. Finally, remove the plasticene from the inside, pad the space with anything to hand, and finish off the back with a piece of firm material glued or stitched. For a brooch, add a safety-pin; and for a ring, a short piece of elastic stitched on to fit the finger of the wearer. The same principles can be applied using screw-top lids as a base and building up the shape and design in Polyfilla.

For headdresses, tiaras and crowns a shape of wire or cardboard can be used, built up with layers of pasted paper decorated with beads and odd earrings, curtain rings and string, painted with gilt paints. To make beads—used also for necklaces and belts—cut long strips of paper, wider at one end and tapering away to almost nothing at the other end. Roll up the strips, beginning from the larger end and pasting them well as you go. and using a knitting needle as a spindle. When the beads are dry they can be removed from the needle and painted. The size of the beads will be determined by the width and length of the strips of paper used. Carpet binding makes a very good base for belts and jewelled collars, and materials and trimmings can be either glued or stitched to it.

DECORATING FABRIC FOR STAGE COSTUMES: JOAN CHARLTON

When we are decorating fabric for use on the stage, our need is for speed, ease of work and low cost of materials. It is unlikely that the dyes used will need to be stable enough to withstand laundering, but they should be sufficiently stable not to rub off on the skin. The fabric need not stand up to close scrutiny, but it must be effective at a distance. If we bear these points in mind, we shall understand that the *design* is of paramount importance. Large, simple shapes which are effective from a distance are better than small complicated ones, which give a muzzy effect.

There are four main ways of decorating a length of fabric: painting, printing, dyeing and embroidering. Experiment will show the most effective method of gaining the desired result.

Painting
Designs can be painted direct on fabric, using heliyarn dyes or any other suitable fabric ink or paint. An alternative medium, which is cheap and effective, is powder paint mixed with size or PVA. This will not wash, but will stand up to quite heavy use surprisingly well. Experiments need to be carried out on different types of fabric and with different brushes and thicknesses of paint to discover the effects that can be obtained. For example, a thick paint drawn lightly across hessian with a thick brush, can suggest velvet; white paint laid on heavily with a fine brush, can suggest a line of embroidery. Spray paints can also highlight folds and suggest richness of texture, or with cut-out shapes can produce a design.

Printing
Various printing materials can be used to print designs direct on fabrics, e.g. heliyarn dyes, dylon in a polycell base, or powder paint and size. Simple designs can be printed by using vegetable, lino or plasticene blocks; more complicated ones by using silk screens. (Detailed methods of handling printing materials can be found in one of the many books on the subject.)

Dyeing
Resist methods of dyeing can be used to dye designs on lengths of fabric. There are two main methods: (1) tie and dye; and (2) batik.

(1) In the tie-and-dye method, the fabric is tied with string in various ways to produce different effects; for example, a pebble is tied into the fabric to produce a circle, or the fabric can be folded and tied to reproduce stripes. Once the fabric has been tied, it is immersed in a dye bath. The string resists the dye, so that the design appears in the original fabric colour. This process can be repeated with several colours to produce fabric of great richness.

(2) In batik, the design is painted on the fabric in hot paraffin

wax (candle grease). Dye can then be sponged over the cloth or the whole thing can be dipped into a dye bath. The dye runs off the paraffin wax, leaving a clear design. When the fabric is dry, the process can be repeated, using other colours. Finally, the fabric is placed between layers of newspaper and the wax ironed out. Dylon or procion dyes can be used for both these resist methods.

Embroidering

When embroidering designs on to stage costumes, we must remember scale. The work needs to be bold, and we should use thick embroidery materials. Painstaking stitching in fine cottons has little, if any, place on stage costumes. Knitting cottons and yarns are of greater value than stranded silk; large beads show up, while small ones are lost. With any of these methods it is important to stand away from the fabric to check the scale of the work and to view it under stage lights. It can be a sobering experience to realise how much painstaking labour has been wasted because the design is too small to be seen. Finally, in our use of boldness in design we need to remember that it should convey the essence of the period or place, not the detail.

The tasks of making, borrowing, fitting and caring for costumes are supervised by the wardrobe mistress. She first assembles a chart showing the details of the various characters' costumes and the measurements of the actors and actresses who are to play them. Time for fitting costumes must be allocated in the rehearsal schedule and practise costumes are provided when the cast need to gain experience during rehearsal in wearing and moving in unfamiliar types of clothing.

During and after a production costumes have to be carefully stored; cleaning, pressing and repairs are often essential and require a high degree of skill and organisation in addition to extensive knowledge of fabrics and design on the part of the wardrobe mistress.

All objects used on the stage and not part of a costume are known as properties, 'props' for short: these may include small 'hand props' such as fans and canes or very large items like chests or cannons. Generally speaking, the larger or more unusual the property the greater the need for imaginative use of cheap materials. Props must be light enough for easy movement, strong enough to withstand use and must exhibit the correct blend of realism and harmony with other aspects of the production.

Suitable materials will include chicken wire (as a base), foam rubber and plastic, papier mâché, fibreglass, balsawood and polystyrene (which must be cut with a special 'hot wire' tool). It is helpful to build up a collection of useful items for the construction of small props including: yoghurt cups, cotton reels, washing-up liquid containers, sardine-tin openers, lengths of picture cord, curtain rings, buttons and beads.

The 'property mistress' in a production needs to be well organised, scrupulous in the care of borrowed items and on the constant look-out for running repairs. She will make a property plot after her first reading of the text and discussion with the director and designer. Part of a property plot for Anouilh's play *Becket* is shown here:

Prop	Scene	Page	User	Position
Towel	1	7	Page	O.S.L.
Clothes	1	7	Becket & King	On bed S.R.
6 stools	1	11	Councillors	Bring on S.L.
Seal	1	12	King	In pocket
Flagon	1	17	Guard	Bring on S.L.
Hawks	1	19	Becket & King	Keep O.R.
Firewood	1	23	Saxon	Hut U.R.

DISCUSSION AND ACTIVITY

1. Construct a crown to fit one of the members of your group. Use materials suggested in this unit and consult pictures to decide on a 'period'.
2. Read Act IV Scene 1 in Shakespeare's *Richard II*. How does the crown you have made help your acting? One group work on the scene; other groups improvise a scene with a crown as a central feature.
3. How important is absolute historical accuracy? Make some sketches or collect illustrations of costumes worn in the Elizabethan and Restoration theatre.

BIBLIOGRAPHY

Warren Kenton: *Stage Properties and How to Make Them*, Pitman, London, 1964.

Julia Tompkins: *Stage Costumes*, Pitman, London, 1964.

Motley: *Designing and Making Stage Costumes*, Studio Vista, London, 1964.

Peters and Sutcliffe: *Making Costumes for School Plays*, Batsford, London, 1971.

Sheila Jackson: *Simple Stage Costumes and How to Make Them*, Studio Vista, London, 1968.

Unit 7

Improvisation: *The Death of Grass*

The novel *The Death of Grass* by John Christopher describes an alarming event: because of a virus originating in China all grass-like vegetation in the world begins to die. Crops which form the staple diet of men and cattle wither, and no remedy can be found.

This idea is the basis of the extended improvisation which comprises this unit.

DISCUSSION AND ACTIVITY

1. What are the likely implications of a crisis of this magnitude?
2. In large groups develop a 'dance drama' showing the gradual advance of a destructive force and the nature of man's reaction to it.

OR

3. In small groups decide how the danger might be recog-

nised and choose roles to play in the situation. Consider: what regulations might be enforced; how people behave when survival is their main aim; how could *you* survive in this situation?

Try now to make a play including the results of your discussion—build scenes with clearly defined climaxes and aim for an ending of considerable impact. Music may help —especially the dry sounds of percussion, a single drum beat or the rattle of a tambourine.

4. Obtain the novel and compare your version with the original: John Christopher: *The Death of Grass*, Penguin, Harmondsworth, 1970.

'Let Her Paint an Inch Thick!'

'Make-up' is usually defined as a collection of lipsticks, powders, creams, eyebrow pencils etc. which women use to enhance the appearance of their faces and bodies. A little research shows that the use of make-up is by no means limited to women. Zulu warriors, Red Indians, eighteenth-century gentlemen and some twentieth-century males also employ cosmetics either to make themselves more fierce as in the case of the Zulus and Indians or more attractive as with the men of the eighteenth and twentieth centuries, of whom the latter may use tanning cream, talcum powder, wigs or hairpieces to improve their appearance.

The choice of make-up, its appearance and application are important in everyday life. A walk through a crowded shopping centre will give you plenty of examples of make-up subtly or crudely applied. People will be wearing make-up for different purposes; to hide facial defects, attract attention to themselves or conform with the latest 'way out' fashion. Perhaps it gives a sense of security when the true 'self' is hidden.

A colour scheme in make-up may blend with nails, shoes and clothes, or create a sense of shock by violently contrasting colours or tones. The basic intention with all uses is a disguise of some kind.

'The smell of the grease paint' is a phrase that is often

used to convey the excitement of the theatre. Make-up plays an important part in theatrical presentations extending far beyond the desire for cosmetic improvement. Character, nationality, different moods can all be suggested by careful make-up. The ageing of Eric Porter in *The Forsyte Saga* and Keith Michell in *The Six Wives of Henry VIII* was achieved through skilfully planned application.

In general, theatrical make-up is used for the following reasons:

(*a*) To compensate for the high intensity of artificial light under which the actor or actress works.
(*b*) To highlight the eyes: the most expressive part of the body.
(*c*) To change the appearance.
(*d*) Possibly to impart a deliberate formalisation to the appearance.

Recent developments in staging and acting styles have had a considerable effect upon theatrical make-up and suggestions contained in the older textbooks are sometimes out of date. It is very important that the audience are not aware of obvious crudely applied make-up. Subtlety and care are essential in the planning and application of stage make-up. This is achieved by practice and observation under stage lighting conditions.

The books listed in the bibliography at the end of the unit give detailed advice on make-up methods. They depend on starting from a clean base. It is important to remove every-day make-up first.

A good deal of heat is generated by stage lighting and the wearing of heavy stage costume. This may lead to excessive perspiration on the face and body. It is essential for some kind of deodorant or anti-perspirant to be used by both men and women to avoid damage to the costume and embarrassment to fellow actors.

DISCUSSION AND ACTIVITY

1. Be aware of the particular nature of your own skin, e.g. dryness or sensitivity. Take this into account when applying

make-up. Examine your own face carefully so that you understand its bone structure, skin condition etc.

2. Use the make-up books for reference. Apply a make-up that you think appropriate for a character of your own age and appearance on the stage.

3. Experiment with methods of (*i*) making yourself older, (*ii*) expressing a very dominant characteristic, e.g. surly, exotic, unwell, (*iii*) making a clown or animal face.

4. Make a collection of photographs for reference showing faces that vividly express feelings, age, nationality, attitudes. Notice how their expressions are achieved by line, shadow or shape.

5. Study the photograph in this unit which shows Joanna David (well known from BBC TV's *The Last of the Mohicans* and *War and Peace*), Cynthia Grenville, Richard Gale,

Plate IV   *Photograph: Arthur Palmer, courtesy Kentish Gazette*

Maria Warburg and Valerie Georgeson in Ibsen's *A Doll's House* at the Marlowe Theatre, Canterbury. What contribution does make-up add to the quality of the faces? Discuss how you think the appearance was achieved.

BIBLIOGRAPHY

Philippe Perrottet: *Practical Stage Make-Up*, Studio Vista, London, 1967.
Eric Jones: *Make-Up for School Plays*, Batsford, London, 1969.
Harold Melvill: *The Magic of Make-Up*, Barrie & Rockcliff, London, 1966.
Jack Stuart Knapp: *The Technique of Stage Make-Up* (available from Messrs Samuel French).

Unit 9

'Let There Be Light'
—an Act of Creation!

The Ancient Greeks saw their plays in the light of a Mediter-
ranean dawn; the Elizabethans and Jacobeans watched
Shakespeare under the skies of London (what Hamlet
called 'that excellent canopy the air'). The Victorians
revelled in the possibilities of gaslight. One particular type,
'the limelight', still survives as a figure of speech. We are
now able to achieve a control and great variety of light in the
theatre undreamed of even one hundred years ago.

Such is the potential of modern stage lighting as a part of
the total impact of a theatrical experience that it must form
an ingredient of the director's and designer's conception
and planning. Yet it is surprising how often the lighting of
an amateur production is a disorganised afterthought
which draws attention to itself by its inefficiency. Even the
most simple equipment can contribute valuably to drama if
used with skill and adequate rehearsal.

To some extent the increased potential in direction,
intensity and colour has altered the nature of writing for the
theatre.

Theatrical lighting can achieve:

1. *Maximum visibility*—it is important for the audience to
be able to see without difficulty and this, strangely enough,
helps them to hear! Eyes and facial expressions must usually
be visible.

2. *Highlighting*—the director can draw attention to certain
points and play others down by focusing the lighting upon
particular parts of the stage, leaving others in darkness.

3. *Atmosphere*—the intangible quality. The particular
mood of a scene, e.g. sadness, gaiety, can be suggested by
subtle use of light and colour.

4. *Illusion*—the use of projections, gauzes, blackouts, ultraviolet lanterns and stroboscopic lights can create exciting effects.

The main types of lantern used today fall in three categories: spotlights, floodlights and special effects lanterns.

Spotlights

A lamp (usually 250–1,000 watts) is encased in a lantern which contains a highly polished reflector. The light passes through a lens and becomes an intense beam which can be altered in spread and direction. Spotlights are hung (*a*) above the auditorium when they are known as Front of House (F.O.H.) lights, (*b*) on a barrel above the stage, (*c*) high at either side of the stage (perches). They may also be mounted on stands in any part of the theatre.

The *Profile* spotlight, which has a smooth lens, throws a hard-edged beam which falls on to the stage as a clearly defined ellipse of light, capable of ranging in size from a pinpoint sufficient to illumine an actor's face to an area some six feet across. Perhaps the most obvious example of the *Profile* is the 'follow spot' which lights a champion ice-skater.

The ridged lens *Fresnel* spotlight produces a soft-edged beam—the effect on the stage is of an area of light which decreases gradually and fades imperceptibly at the edges. In order to control the spread of light more accurately these lanterns are often fitted with shutters known as 'barn-doors' which are often visible on BBC TV's *Top of the Pops* and similar shows. The 500-watt *Fresnel* and a larger version, the 1,000-watt *Pageant*, are particularly suitable for various types of studio work because of the natural quality of light they produce at short range and the ease with which it can be blended.

Floodlights

The floodlight is a lamp enclosed in a metal box with one open side. A reflector may be fitted and quite an efficient substitute for a commercially produced lantern can be made

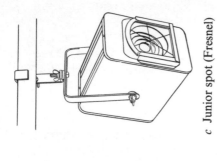

c Junior spot (Fresnel)

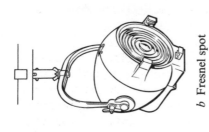

b Fresnel spot

Figure 4a Profile spot

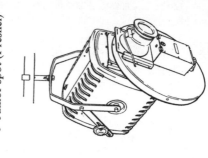

Figure 5 Optical effects illuminates

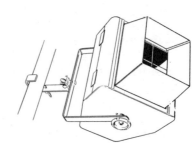

e Flood with masking hood

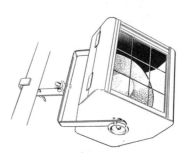

d Floodlight

Credit for Figs 4 and 5: Courtesy Rank Strand Electric

by installing a 250-watt bulb in one of the large tins in which plums etc. are delivered to school and college canteens! Floodlighting gives a general wash of light over a large area and is used to supplement spotlighting (often with colour) and to light cycloramas and scene-backings and to provide footlights. These lanterns may be seen in groups above the stage when they are known as 'battens' or standing on the stage angled upwards to light the cyclorama as a 'ground row'; the spread of light from a floodlight can be restricted somewhat by fitting a 'masking hood' and a waterproof floodlight is now manufactured.

Special effects lanterns

These include rain, hail, snow and cloud projectors which operate by a glass disc in which markings have been made rotating between a 1,000-watt lamp and a high-definition lens. There are also stroboscopic flashing lights, overhead and back projection techniques for scenery, and 'Linnebach' lanterns which throw a shadowy image on to the cyclorama.

Colour

A frame containing a sheet of coloured 'cinemoid' can be slotted over the aperture of any lantern. The following colours are now available:

Lavender–Gold–Pink

Pale Violet	42	Pink	57
Pale Lavender	36	Middle Rose	10
Gold Tint	51	Dark Pink	11
Pale Gold	52	Deep Salmon	8
Pale Salmon	53	Bright Rose	48
Pale Rose	54	Deep Rose	12
Light Salmon	9	Smoky Pink	27
Light Rose	7	Magenta	13

Yellow–Amber–Red

Pale Yellow	50	Deep Salmon	8
Straw	3	Apricot	47
Yellow	1	Orange	5
Canary	49	Deep Orange	5A
Light Amber	2	Deep Golden Amber	35
Medium Amber	4	Pale Red	66

Chrome Yellow	46	Primary Red	6
Deep Amber	33	Ruby	14
Golden Amber	34		

Blue–Purple–Violet

Turquoise	62	Bright Blue	41
Blue–Green (Cyan)	16	Slate Blue	61
Peacock Blue	15	Medium Blue	32
Steel Tint	67	Sky Blue	63
Steel Blue	17	Dark Blue	19
Daylight	45	Deep Blue	20
Pale Blue	40	Purple	25
Pale Navy Blue	43	Mauve	26
Light Blue	18	Pale Violet	42

Green–Neutral–Frost

Pale Green	38	Peacock Blue	15
Pea Green	21	Chocolate Tint	55
Moss Green	22	Pale Chocolate	56
Light Green	23	Pale Grey	60
Dark Green	24	Light Frost	31
Primary Green	39	Heavy Frost	29
Blue–Green (Cyan)	16	Clear	30
Turquoise	62		

Other colours may be achieved by mixing; but it must be remembered that in dealing with light it is red, blue and green which are the primaries to be combined to produce white.

Firelight, sunlight, moonlight, twilight, sunset and candlelight are the more commonplace of the many illusions which can be created; but the director also has at his disposal the whole range of emotional associations which are revealed when, for instance, we talk of 'warm' and 'cold' colours, 'soft' and 'hard', 'gentle' and 'lurid', 'having the blues' or 'seeing red'. But colour must not be thought of in isolation; it must involve harmony with the décor, costumes, make-up and properties.

Control
Modern stage lighting is controlled through a 'dimmer board' which enables lanterns to be switched or faded on or off at any required speed. The most recent and sophisticated lighting controls resemble an Organ Console and the

positioning of the 'lighting box' (where the technician operates the lights) at the rear of the auditorium has greatly simplified the designer's task.

It is clearly beyond the scope of this book to give detailed information or instruction in stage lighting: your ability to follow up this outline of modern trends will depend on access to expensive equipment of many possible designs. You should, however, have gained some impression of the almost infinite number of subtle or startling changes of visual effect which are now possible in the theatre and realise the need for imagination and restraint, careful planning and striving for balance that are vital.

DISCUSSION AND ACTIVITY

1. If you have access to lighting equipment, experiment with separate lights and discover what effects can be achieved by (*i*) adjusting the focus, (*ii*) the use of colour frames, (*iii*) the use of 'irises' or 'barn-doors', (*iv*) re-positioning the lantern, (*v*) varying its intensity. Remember that you judge the appropriateness of the lighting source by its effectiveness in illuminating an object or person. With two lanterns a considerable variety of effects can be achieved. Take a simple object like a football and light it in as many different ways as possible; notice how the appearance of the object changes as varying qualities and directions of light illumine it.

2. For 'end' staging F.O.H. spotlights should normally operate in pairs, lighting areas of the stage from both sides of the auditorium. Try rigging two spotlights to light one area—angle the lanterns down at 45 degrees, the main beams should meet at 90 degrees to each other.

3. Each change of lighting is a cue; cues should be numbered and entered in the director's 'prompt copy'—but whereas the director may write: '3. A pale grey sky against which figures are silhouetted' the lighting technician will write details of the lanterns which are to be faded in to achieve this effect.

4. On your next visit to the theatre notice the sources of light.

5. Look up 'Lighting' in the *Oxford Companion to the Theatre* and trace its development.
6. What colours might create various moods in the theatre?
7. Contact Rank Strand Electric Ltd, at 29 King Street, London, W.C.2; obtain their *Tabs Lighting Compendium* and avail yourself of the other services offered.
8. Why is the lighting control box best positioned at the rear of the auditorium?

BIBLIOGRAPHY

Peter Goffin: *Stage Lighting for Amateurs*, Garnet Miller, London, 1955.
Geoffrey Ost: *Stage Lighting*, Herbert Jenkins, London, 1957.
National Federation of Women's Institutes: *Focus on Drama*, 1968.
    (This, the best simple guide to the use of lighting equipment, includes excellent advice on lighting 'in the round'.)

Unit 10

Design for the Theatre

Theatre design is a specialised branch of visual art which requires an extensive knowledge of drama as well as great executive skill; it involves the design of settings and costumes for plays, operas and shows of every conceivable variety.

Almost alone among artists the theatre designer must work within already established and clearly defined limits: the size of the stage and a budget. But the dimensions involved and the wide choice of materials allow for vast imaginative scope.

ACTIVITY

1. Now study the illustrations in this unit. They show the sketch and model for the setting of Arthur Schnitzler's play *The Green Cockatoo* made by the young designer Susan ffitch. In the passage which follows we see how the designer approaches his task and then gives detailed instructions on the making of a model set.

How the design changes from sketch to model
Having read the play and discussed it with the director, the designer's next job is to describe the characters and settings in visual terms. Initially he must create an atmosphere in which the play can take place. Ignoring technical details he will produce a number of sketches for the set until he feels he has achieved the 'right' atmosphere; at this point he can begin to define walls, stairs, various levels, etc. on the drawing, ready to transfer these to the ground plan—this is where the translation from two dimensions into three

Plates v and vi

begins, in other words the moment at which a drawn shape is lifted off the sketch and made into a three-dimensional piece in the model. Within this process the designer often finds that certain ideas he had in the set drawing are not technically possible. For example, the sketch for the setting of *The Green Cockatoo* contained ideas which were found impractical when made up in the model. The stairs were moved farther downstage and positioned at a right angle to the side wall, instead of curving them forward from farther back as intended in the sketch. The shape of the ceiling had to be changed radically. It was lowered and arched with the side and back walls divided to lessen their height. More contours were added. The play takes place in a Parisian cellar at the end of the eighteenth century. Whilst the sketch provided the right atmosphere it did not create a sufficiently intimate setting suggestive of an underground cellar. The model provides the opportunity to oppose and juxtapose various parts of the set until the right combination is found. Different widths and heights of card are tied together with colours and textures. Because all the pieces can be moved and adjusted easily, the technical problems are solved at this point.

How to go about making a model
The designer is given a ground plan (a bird's eye view of the stage) and an elevation (a view of the stage as if you were looking through the side wall or the wings). From these he works out where he will place his set on the stage, the scale of the plan is usually $\frac{1}{2}'' = 1'$ (in other words $\frac{1}{2}$ inch on a ruler represents 1 foot in reality). This means that using the same scale he can measure from the two plans the width and depth of the stage, the points at which the lighting barrels and fly bars are hung above the stage, the height of the proscenium arch (if one exists); in fact from this he can establish all the knowledge he needs to make a model.

The basic materials needed are strong card (black one side, white the other, $\frac{1}{8}''$ thick), a Stanley knife, a metal ruler, a tube of impact adhesive glue and a packet of drawing pins. The designer first makes a model box. This is done by cutting out the stage floor, the side and back walls, the fly

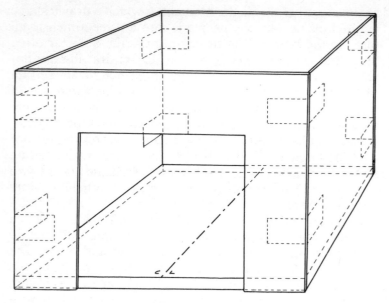

Fig. 6

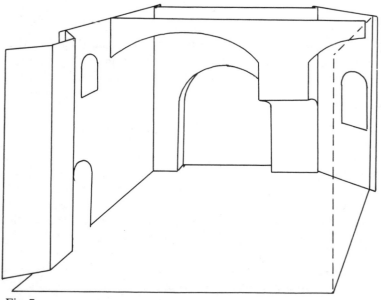

Fig. 7

Fig. 8

Fig. 9

galleries and the proscenium arch using the black side of the card. These are then glued together and made secure by adding small cardboard hinges at all corners of the box (see Fig. 6). He can then begin to cut his own set pieces using the same scale and the white side of the card; a scale figure must also be cut out, as all the set pieces relate back to the human scale. You will see from Fig. 7 the basic cardboard pieces which were cut out using a Stanley knife and a metal ruler for *The Green Cockatoo*. These were assembled temporarily in the model, using masking tape and various jars and boxes to prop them up from behind. The walls could not be fixed permanently at this point as they had to be removed and added to, in terms of building up the structure more and adding texture and colour.

The next step was to add the cardboard beams, see Fig. 8, in other words the large raised areas and then to add the smaller structural shapes, see Fig. 9; this meant using matchsticks for the wall surfaces and doors and small pieces of shaped card for the door surrounds and floor tiling.

All the structural and raised areas on the model have been established with card or matchsticks and the set is ready to be textured and painted. The effect of cellar walls was achieved by mixing Polyfilla in different consistencies, applying it to the card with a knife and then working back into it with a knife end and the end of a pencil just before the Polyfilla had set firm. Perhaps the most satisfying job of all is the final painting of the set; Polyfilla is porous and therefore holds poster colour well. The paint was applied like the Polyfilla in various thick and thin consistencies emphasising some areas and shading others.

The furniture was carved out of $\frac{1}{4}''$ balsawood and textured and coloured in the same way as the model.

There are often other materials involved—gauze and net for gauzes, calico for projection screens, card with paper (coloured or textured) stuck on for flats, backcloths and borders, plastics such as melinex, tinfoil—in fact ideas can develop from many inanimate objects and materials.

2. Make a collection of photos or drawings of stage settings from magazines or newspapers. Try to discover the methods of construction and the materials used.

Pay special attention to the play setting on your next theatre visit. If possible arrange a backstage visit to see the actual scenery and the carpenters' and painters' workshops.
3. There are several play extracts or full texts in this book. Select one of them and try to devise a set using the suggestions made in this unit. Include ideas for colour and furnishing.
4. Many television programmes including plays, shows and discussion programmes take place in carefully designed settings. Select three of these programmes: notice the settings and assess their effectiveness.
5. Look at the different stage designs in Unit 3. Discuss the adaptation of your designs to suit the shape of the acting area. Each stage shape makes its own special demands in design. Try to decide from your discussion what these demands are.
6. Not all plays employ realistic settings. Sometimes designers use abstract or 'symbolic' settings to suggest the locations. Notice in your collection of illustrations the style that the designer has adopted.
7. If you listed all the locations in a Shakespeare play, it would appear impossible to create a separate setting for each different scene. In a production of *Macbeth* at the National Theatre the whole action was set against a permanent structure representing a granite wall and massive doorways. If you have the opportunity to use a drama studio, try to devise some settings using rostra and lights. You might focus on the idea of a doorway, a small enclosed room (a cellar or attic) or an outdoor courtyard or market square. Improvise or set scenes that utilise these settings. (Several of the play texts referred to in this book will be useful, e.g. *The Long and the Short and the Tall*, *Luther*, *In Committee*.)

BIBLIOGRAPHY

Phyllis Hartnoll (ed.): *The Oxford Companion to the Theatre*, OUP, London, 1967. Contains 150 illustrations of various aspects of design.
Edward Craig: *Gordon Craig*, Gollancz, London, 1969.
   The work of an influential designer considered.

Peter Chilver and Eric Jones: *Designing a School Play*, Batsford, London, 1968.

Eric Jones: *Stage Construction for Stage Plays*, Batsford, London, 1969.

Stephen Joseph: *Scene Painting and Design*, Pitman, London, 1964.

Kenneth Rowell: *Stage Design*, Studio Vista, London, 1968.

Michael Warre: *Designing and Making Stage Scenery*, Studio Vista, London, 1966.

Plays and Players, October, November and December 1969, issues featured a series 'The Designer Talks'. Many libraries keep back numbers.

Compelling look at prejudice

LEICESTER AUTHOR David Campton's half-hour play, **Incident**, shown on B.B.C. 1 last night — it was screened on B.B.C. 2 in January this year — was a well-conceived and effective piece of comment on segregation.

TIME AND TIDE 16 MARCH 1961

... is going to build him one, and at
...'s more—of the

Leicester Mercury
Head Office: St. George Street,
Leicester (Telephone: 20451).
London Office:
44, Fleet Street, E.C.4

Last night's theatre

Enjoyment in infectious in players' romp

DAVID CAMPTON'S new plays
... in The Round last night ...
first performance at Scarborough ...
... milling time with the players ...
... Rates: 3 months 13s. 6d.
... romped through these paces with ...
an infectious joyous enjoyment.

Theatre by *Richard Findlater*

HE STAGE

ESTABLISHED 1880

EDITOR:
Eric Joh'

ces: 19-21 Tavistock Street
Telephones: Temple I
Telegrams: The Stage, Rand,
n Rates: 3 months 13s. 0d
2s. 0d. Single 1s. 1s

THE STAR, SHEFFIELD, Tuesday, June 13, 1972.

Terrific impact of vampire thriller

easy to see why the author, David Camp'
was awarded an Arts Council bursary
years ago. This state grant enabled ...
ton, a 37-year-old former gas board ...
to concentrate on writing for the stage;
and he is now the only resident dramatist
working for a permanent theatrical group
in Britain, which is another of the significant facts about the play I saw in Heme
Hempstead last week.

Mr Campton joined the Studio Theatre
as an actor three years ago, and since then
he has written a new play each year fo
this company. He has written ...
over, for perform ...

An unusual com
of surprises

GLASGOW HERALD,

OCTOBER 21, 1965

"LITTLE BROTHER—LITTLE SISTER."

by David Campton.

David Campton's post-atomic
fairy-tale is different ... mutter.
Echoes of Lewis Carroll as well as
Grimm, not to mention Genesis,
go to make up this odd touching,
funny, and beautiful story of the
world getting ready to be born
again 20 years after the last day.
But, being a true fairy-tale,
is not all sentiment. Cook,
the faithful old tyrant who rules
the roost down there in the secure
shelter, is a real ogress,
or naughty children she will mince,
truly as sharp as a razor; and
Adam and Eve, Hansel and Gretel,
of the radiation-proof gingerbread
house, are really growing into man
and woman.

Fourteen Delightful
Views of Life

FOURTEEN delightful views of
life, seven players, no plot—
and actor-playwright David Campton's "Out of Studio Theatre Limited has
ion of Scarborough playgoers a
good, bright little deed in a world
of entertainment mediocrity.
'y he use of

---

comedy with all the
ifications for success

Was."

Most effective of the ...
nel 13 triple bill was David
Campton's "Out of the Flying
Pan," a savage, scathing at-
tack on the sometime double-
talk of international diplomacy. It was not entirely fair
but absolutely brilliant in conception language, macabre
humor and execution.

In cryptic, punning lan-
guage that was Joycean and
Al Kelly gibberish with touches of Lewis Carroll, two top-
hatted, morning-coated, as-
coted diplomats went through
cycles of platitudes, lies, am-
biguities, boasts and deceits
that led from negotiation to
all-out war.

As played by Alan Alda and
James Ray, the play was ...
spired, malicious no ...
varding an ...
betwe ...

New York Herald Tribune

Comic Surrealis
In One-Act Play

By John Horn

"The New York Television
Theater" last night pre-
sented three interesting, at
times amusing and other
times wildly funny, exercises
in comic surrealism.

Three one-actors, smartly
'roduced and directed by
...an, complemented
... hour of
...

epu) ...
emotional
... sometimes
... savagely
... if a man
... disgust at
... wrong kind
At his best,
... from

... iquely ...
... political and
... nd fantasy as
... akes its point
... d behind the
... pons—one was
... on the Alder-
... s it often with
... he audience at
... nt didn't laugh,
... ide of their faces
... terror—that was
... to weaknesses of
... is due to the

THEATRE GUILD
EXCEL IN
COMEDY-DRAMA

SCARBOROUGH THEATRE GUILD could hardly go
wrong with a play like "The Cactus Garden" on their hands.

Scarbor' Evening News
and Daily Post

Thursday 22 January 1959

Telephone 946

... ...ritain
... he Arts
... shown
... r, he
... and ATV; he has built
... uch local support in Scarborough
...nat the Council nearly built him a theatre;
and he has made such an impression on
Newcastle-under-Lyme that the Council

your da
with th
groups, s
Exercise
to the
from the

The Yorkshire Post

Founded as The Leeds Intelligencer on July 2, 1754,
became a daily, The Yorkshire Post, on July 2, 1866.

Tel: LEEDS 32701 (Advertising only, 36272), LONDON FLE 9693.
LEEDS FRIDAY JULY 31 1964

LAST NIGHT'S THEATRE

PREMIERE IS
A HIT

THE actor-playwright David
Campton has done it again.
Last night the first performance of
his new play Dead and Alive was
given to a capacity audience in
Scarborough's Library Theatre.

Unit 11

A Case Study

In this unit we are going to consider the work of one of the most fascinating contemporary playwrights: David Campton. Since 1956, the year of Suez, the Hungarian Revolution, Rock'n' Roll and John Osborne's *Look Back in Anger*, an increasing number of young writers have turned to plays as a means of expressing their view of the world and the problems of existence. Encouraged by the opportunities of television, the atmosphere of receptiveness to experimental ideas in the Theatre and the success of writers like Brecht and Beckett, these new playwrights have produced disturbing and, at times, puzzling drama.

David Campton began work with the Midland Gas Board, but became associated with the Theatre in the Round at Scarborough where Stephen Joseph was director (see Unit 3).

In his plays, Campton concerns himself with some of the forces which threaten us either from outside—such as dictatorships and authority—or from deep within our subconscious. These forces are not specifically identified, but are represented in symbolic, often apparently absurd, images of striking originality. His plays are often comic in style, but threatening in their concepts. They may be termed 'Comedies of Menace' of which *Then* and *The Cage Birds* are good examples.

Then depicts the two lone survivors of a nuclear war: a middle-aged schoolmaster and Miss Europe, both having survived because they remembered to put paper bags over their heads. They face the future together, wondering whether to remove their bags!

The situation is typical of the comic tragedy which makes

Campton's writing so immediate in its impact and yet so lingering in the memory.

DISCUSSION AND ACTIVITY

1. Here now is the cast list and introductory note for a recent play, *The Cage Birds*, together with the programme note which David Campton wrote for a private performance of the play by students at Hereford College of Education where he was a visiting lecturer in 1971.

An author should never write a programme note, because writing a play is the equivalent of dreaming in public: and if we took to analysing our own dreams, what would the psychiatrists do for a living? I only know that lately my dreams have been invaded by birds. I cannot say what this means, but merely state the fact that, through some crack or loophole in my subconscious at least one of our feathered friends has found a way into my last four plays. This is puzzling, because I know next to nothing about birds—only that if one keeps very still, in time they will either go away or nest in one's hair. Of course I could try to drive them out of my plays, but until now I have hesitated—once the birds have gone, who knows what may take their place? Caterpillars perhaps, and I hate caterpillars. (This is, I believe, what ecology is all about.) However, while the Freudians are having a field-day, the rest of the audience may prefer to enjoy the plays. Each part of the programme is a comedy. You may note that the first half is comic with sad overtones; while the second half is sad with comic overtones. Which, without being a psychiatrist, is as far as anyone can analyse a play.

CAST

THE LONG-TONGUED GOSSIP

THE MIRROR-EYED GAZER

THE MEDICATED GLOOM

THE REGULAR THUMP

THE CONSTANT TWITTING

THE GREAT GUZZLER

THE WILD ONE

THE MISTRESS

The action takes place in a room with a single large door.

Note
Although no character is based on a specific bird, they should have bird-like characteristics, particularly in movement. Bird-like appendages should be translated into human terms: there should be no beaks or plumage, but a long beak, for instance, could be indicated by a walking stick, or extravagant plumage by a fan. Although each bird seems to have its own particular song, the intent behind the words should be made plain. It is possible to say 'pass the salt' aggressively, longingly, with passion or fear: so with these speeches, even though the meaning of the scene cuts across the words.

The first six characters have been in the room for an unspecified period of time; each obsessed with her own predicament they have developed particular traits which give rise to self-centred chatter. They talk at each other but never listen; their sensitivity to any situation has been reduced. Suddenly 'The Mistress' unlocks the door and pushes in 'The Wild One' who desperately tries to incite the other inmates to rebellion. Pleas for careful listening, eloquence, reasoning—all fail. When the triumphant 'Wild

One' successfully picks the lock nobody will venture outside. The prison has become a home: closed minds are more comfortable than new ideas.

At the end of the play the 'birds' are for once united in the destruction of the 'Wild One'—they have murdered their saviour.

Use these ideas as the basis for an Improvisation.

Consider situations in which you have played the role of the 'Wild One' and imagine the dangers involved in introducing new ideas—are revolutionaries sometimes merely sowers of discord? Evolve a scene which explores some of these themes.

2. Brecht's play *The Life of Galileo* shows the inventor as a revolutionary in dispute with authority. The 'hero' of *Billy Liar* by Keith Waterhouse is a lad who does not conform to convention. Pip, the central figure of *Chips with Everything*, rebels against his training in the RAF. There is a scene in which Sir Thomas More, in *A Man for all Seasons*, is a nonconformist. Study these plays: select scenes for reading or acting and discover how the playwright deals with the problem of 'Revolution', 'The Outsider', 'The Wild One'. Are the views presented biased or balanced?

Unit 12

In Committee

Contemporary sociologists and philosophers are investigating the use of language and revealing serious deficiencies in our ability to communicate effectively. This concern is shared by modern playwrights like Pinter and Ionesco.

The more formal the situation in which we find ourselves the more we retreat behind an acquired jargon. Campton's play *Out of the Flying Pan* is a ruthless exposure of the language of international diplomacy but in the new play which comprises this unit he turns his attention to the 'Committee'.

1. Read the play. *Note*: A successful reading will depend on the effectiveness of the interruptions. The characters must be quick to take their cues. The speeches should almost overlap.

2. How are the officials of any committee or council you know about elected or appointed? Using an example from one of them improvise the election of a new chairman and discuss a vital issue about which members disagree.

3. How does your improvisation compare with Campton's play?

4. Michael Argyle, the social psychologist, describes a committee in the following terms:

. . . a problem-solving and creative group formed to deal with complex problems where a variety of different skills or expertise is needed. The meetings are often infrequent and formal, and consist mainly of talk.

Discuss the meaning of this statement and how this contrasts with other types of human group before reading the play.

Notice how the playwright uses the actor/audience relationship in an unusual way. Your reaction to the play will of course be entirely personal but may depend on how you decide to approach it and of your experience in committees.

When the secondary school girl Sheelagh Delaney saw a play by Terence Rattigan she was so convinced that she could write a better play that she set to work at once. The result was *A Taste of Honey*—one of the most successful plays of our age! If you decide that you can produce a better script than Campton do not hesitate to try.

5. Read Harold Pinter's short play *Black and White*.

How does that dialogue compare with conversations you have heard in cafés, fish and chip bars, or bus queues?

BIBLIOGRAPHY

John Russell Taylor: *Anger and After*, Penguin, Harmondsworth, 1962.
 For a consideration of Campton's work.
David Campton: *Laughter and Fear*, Blackie, Glasgow, 1970.
 An anthology of plays.
The Sixth Windmill Book of One Act Plays, Heinemann, London, 1972.
Theatre Today, Longmans, London, 1962.
 Contains Pinter's *Black and White* and Campton's *Then*.

In Committee

by David Campton

CAST

CHAIRMAN
SECRETARY
TREASURER
HAY
BEE
SEA
MEMBER OF THE AUDIENCE
OTHER MEMBERS OF THE AUDIENCE
(*Note: These parts may be played by either male or female performers*)

SCENE: A Committee Room on a stage

TIME: Now

(*A committee meeting is in progress, with everyone talking at once.*)

CHAIRMAN: Order, please. Please. This is no way to. . . . One at a time if you. . . . Let us all be. . . .

TREASURER: The Balance Sheet is the beginning and end of the question. How does it affect the balance sheet?

SECRETARY: Talking won't alter facts. You can talk until you're blue in the face. Or red, according to your politics. But you can't escape facts.

HAY: I repeat. I say I repeat. If necessary I shall go on repeating.

BEE: I have not yet replied. I appeal to the chair. Do I, or do I not have the right of reply?

SEA: There is a simple answer. There is always a simple answer if one approaches the problem in the spirit of compromise.

(*The* CHAIRMAN *bangs on the table.*)

CHAIRMAN: Order!

    (*Silence falls, which surprises everyone—most of all the* CHAIRMAN.)

CHAIRMAN: We seem to have reached a point in our. . . . At which. . . . Not that I wish to. . . . Frank and open has always been our. . . . Aim straight and trust in The Lord, as my grandfather used to. . . . Or words to that effect. But to sum up. . . .

BEE: You can't.

CHAIRMAN: I beg your—er. . . .

BEE: You can't sum up. We haven't finished.

CHAIRMAN: I was under the impression that I. . . . As Chairman, you understand. When everyone has. . . .

BEE: I haven't.

CHAIRMAN: But you were the first to. . . .

BEE: I don't deny it.

CHAIRMAN: In which case. . . .

BEE: There you are.

TREASURER: Where?

CHAIRMAN: Surely at this point I should. . . . For the benefit of. . . . Before we all. . . . To clarify. . . .

BEE: You sum up after I've answered their objections. That's called right of reply.

CHAIRMAN: Ah, yes. Right of. . . .

BEE: Reply.

SECRETARY: If you agree to that there'll be no time for anything else this week.

BEE: I'm quite aware of the Secretary's opposition to my proposal.

SECRETARY: I'm not opposing it. I'll vote for it. I'll vote for anything to get this meeting moving. We've talked backwards, forwards, and all the way round the point. If the topic isn't exhausted, I am. I propose that the question be now put.

CHAIRMAN: Ah, you mean that a vote be. . . .

BEE: You can't do that.

CHAIRMAN: Can't I?

SECRETARY: You're the Chairman. You have the authority. Exercise it.

CHAIRMAN: The motion before the meeting is—er. . . .

SECRETARY: That the question be now put.

CHAIRMAN: I believe you are all aware of. . . . Naturally my own are. . . . Which I hope is taken for. . . . I therefore. . . .

BEE: The question before us is 'To vote or not to vote'. I have a word to say about that.

TREASURER: Oh, Lord!

BEE: Does anyone deny my right to speak on the motion before the meeting?

SECRETARY: Most of us have homes. Some of us want to get to them.

BEE: I am cognisant of the attitude taken up in some quarters.

SECRETARY: Oh, get on with it.

BEE: Very well. With your permission?

(*The* CHAIRMAN *shrugs feebly.* BEE *stands.* SEA *sits back with eyes closed.*)

SECRETARY: Do you have to stand?

BEE: I think better on my feet.

SECRETARY: Strange where some people keep their brains.

TREASURER: The Time!

BEE: I'll be no longer than it takes to say what I have to say. I'm not one of those who talk for the sake of talking. 'Stand up. Speak up. Shut up.' That's always been my practice.

(HAY *turns away from the table with a sigh of boredom.*)

BEE: I only speak when I've something to say, but when I've something to say, I say it. I'll not be shut up. I've no doubt there are some present who would like to try. To them I can only say. . . .

(*Just about to turn back to the table* HAY *notices the audience.*)

BEE: Out of deference to the Chair, and the nature of this occasion, I'll not say it. But I will have my say.

(HAY *shrugs off the phenomenon, and turns back to the meeting.*)

BEE: Never let it be said that I stood down when it was time to speak up. 'Speak the truth and shame the Devil', I've always said.

(HAY *glances tentatively over shoulder to check that original impression.*)

BEE: What I've said, I've said, and I've always been one to stand by what I've said. Has anybody here known me to go back on what I've said? If anyone says 'yes' they're. . . . Out of deference to the Chair, and the nature of this occasion, I'll not say what.

(HAY *takes a quick glance over the other shoulder at the audience.*)

BEE: I've always been one to say what's on my mind. 'Without fear or favour.' I've said it before, and I'll say it again. 'Without fear or favour.'

(HAY *takes a longer look at the audience, then turns back to the meeting.*)

BEE: So everybody knows where I stand. And if there's anybody who doubts what I say, they can. . . . But out of deference to the Chair, and considering the nature of this meeting, I'll not say what.

(HAY *turns and stares at the audience.*)

BEE: But what I have to say is this. . . .

(BEE *pauses and stares at* HAY. *There is a pause which grows.*)

BEE: Perhaps I am boring the member opposite.

(HAY *turns back to the meeting, apologetic and flustered.*)

HAY: No, no. Not at all. I was about to say the same.

(*Has final glance at the audience.*)

BEE: In which case perhaps we. . . . (*Notices the audience.*) Perhaps we can. . . . We can. . . . Thank you.

(*Suddenly sits, rather shaken.*)

SECRETARY: Will somebody suggest how to minute that?

TREASURER: Does it matter? We talk and talk, but all that counts in the end is the Balance Sheet. The rest is. . . .

(BEE *sneaks a look at the audience. The* TREASURER *follows the direction of the glance, and dries up.*)

TREASURER: Is. . . . Is. . . .

SECRETARY: Is the member for or against the motion? That is all I want to know. A simple yes or no. It. . . .

(*The* SECRETARY *turns to see what the others are looking at, and stares at the audience. The* SECRETARY, *the* TREASURER, HAY *and* BEE *are now all looking at the audience.* SEA *is lost in thought and the* CHAIRMAN *is unaware of anything except the growing silence. Eventually the* CHAIRMAN *decides that the time must have come to sum up.*)

CHAIRMAN: Has everyone quite. . . ? Splendid. In which case we can. . . . Does anyone wish to. . . ? No one? Splendid. Splendid.

TREASURER: Strange.

HAY: Has it ever happened before?

BEE: Not to my knowledge.

CHAIRMAN: Ah, but it was bound to. Hope springs, you know. I was quite sure that if we put our shoulders, and all pushed. . . .

(*The others take no notice.*)

HAY: Well?

BEE: What now?

SECRETARY: I propose that nothing be said.

TREASURER: Can nothing ever be said?

HAY: It's a problem.

SECRETARY: Not yet. It has not been put into words.

HAY: What does. . . ?

BEE: How does. . . ?

TREASURER: We've all. . . .

SECRETARY: Ssh! A problem that is put into words has to be faced. This situation has not yet been put into words. Therefore it does not exist. A problem that does not exist is no problem.

TREASURER: Surely we can't ignore. . . .

SECRETARY: I saw nothing relevant to these proceedings. Did you?

HAY (*doubtfully*): No.

BEE (*decisively*): No.

TREASURER (*coming round to the idea*): No. Nothing.

SECRETARY: Then nothing need be said. Nothing. Nothing.

(*The* CHAIRMAN *is completely baffled.*)

CHAIRMAN: I confess I am somewhat. . . . To say the least of it. I may even be. . . . Perhaps someone would care to put me in the. . . .

SECRETARY: We were about to take a vote. 'That the question be now put.'

CHAIRMAN: You took the words right out of my. . . . All in favour?

(*Everyone except* SEA *says 'Aye'.*)

CHAIRMAN: Against?

(*There is no response.*)

SECRETARY: Sea! Are you against, are you abstaining, or are you asleep?

SEA (*suddenly awake*): Oh. Has Bee finished? I agree, of course. Every time.

SECRETARY (*acidly*): You agree!

SEA: Unless the rest of you are against the idea. I don't want to dissent. There's nothing more disruptive than dissension.

CHAIRMAN: United we. . . .

SEA: Though why should you imagine I was asleep?

TREASURER: It makes no difference.

SEA: One doesn't have to gaze mesmerised at the speaker all the time. One keeps one's mind alert. One draws patterns in the margins of one's agenda paper. One's glance flickers from light fittings to wall coverings to. . . .

(SEA*'s outflung arm points to the audience. For a second the arm seems to hover, then flops down. Looks of consternation flash between all the others except the* CHAIRMAN.)

SEA: But— They. . . .

SECRETARY: We are over here.

SEA: They're. . . .

SECRETARY: A vote will now be taken on the previous question.

SEA: What. . . ?

SECRETARY: That is not the previous question.

SEA: I can—

SECRETARY: We have business to transact here. Here. Here.

SEA: Why should. . . ?

SECRETARY: Indulge in metaphysical speculation in your own time. We have decisions to make.

SEA: But I tell you. . . .

SECRETARY: Perhaps the Chair will call the member to order.

CHAIRMAN: Eh?

SECRETARY: Order.

CHAIRMAN: I wasn't aware. . . . But then I seldom. . . . Or so I'm told. You were saying?

SECRETARY: Instruct the member to confine all observations to the item under discussion.

SEA: It's never happened before.

SECRETARY: We have agreed. Tacitly perhaps. Without discussion maybe. But we have agreed.

SEA: They shouldn't be. . . .

SECRETARY: Be careful what you say. I repeat—a problem that is put into words has to be faced.

SEA: You agreed to sweep it under the carpet?

SECRETARY: A problem that does not exist cannot be swept anywhere. Is that agreed?

TREASURER: Agreed.

HAY: Agreed.

BEE: Agreed.

SECRETARY: And you always agree. The Chairman will now. . . .

SEA: There's a time and place for everything. They were never intended to intrude.

SECRETARY: Nothing has been noted. Now if only the Chairman. . . .

CHAIRMAN: I was just about to suggest that. . . .

SEA: I didn't agree.

TREASURER: You would have done if you'd been awake. You always agree.

SEA: I want to know what they are doing there.

TREASURER: Nothing. Nothing acts except what is actual.

SECRETARY: Nothing can do nothing.

SEA: I'm not blind.

SECRETARY: I almost wish you were dumb.

BEE: If I might say a word. . . .

SECRETARY: It is out of order. There is a motion on the table. All discussion is out of order until a vote has been taken. If the Chairman was up to the job. . . .

CHAIRMAN: Really! *Honi soit qui mal y pense.* As we say in. . . .

SECRETARY: On a point of procedure no one else may speak until a vote has been taken.

SEA: What is there is there.

SECRETARY: That statement is out of order and therefore invalid. I shall not enter it in the minutes, therefore it was never made.

SEA: You can't pretend. They're too solid. They may not belong, but they can't be ignored. Rows of them.

SECRETARY: Words, words, words. If only you realised the damage words can do you'd be more careful how you scatter them.

SEA: Words aren't people.

SECRETARY: Words describe. Words create. Without words nothing can exist. For goodness sake control your words.

SEA: I'm confused.

HAY: That's better.

SEA: And afraid.

SECRETARY: That's worse.

SEA: You know. You wouldn't react like startled rabbits if you didn't know. You know what I know.

SECRETARY: That's enough!

HAY: Please. Let me. . . . You're a good, kind soul, Sea. A tender-hearted listener, and a dab hand with a pot of tea.

SEA: Decent of you to say so.

HAY: But your best friends would never insist that you were quick on the uptake.

SEA: Brains aren't everything.

HAY: Who said they were? Everybody to their job. Just carry on spreading your sympathy, making your tea, and leave thinking to the experts.

SEA: Haven't you grasped what is happening?

SECRETARY: You can take it for granted that we have grasped everything that you have grasped—and are one step ahead.

SEA: Natural order is breaking up.

HAY: I doubt it. But even if it were you could do nothing about the situation. Leave matters as they are.

SEA: This is an emergency. There should be a debate.

SECRETARY: This is a meeting—properly convened, organised, and constituted. And it is high time the Chairman called it to order.

CHAIRMAN: Order?

SECRETARY: Order.

CHAIRMAN (*rapping on the table*): Order. Order.

SEA: Don't be absurd. Order has gone by the board. We can see Them.

SECRETARY: You are out of order.

SEA: If They are possible, anything is possible.

SECRETARY: You are out of order.

SEA: There is no longer any boundary between fact and fiction.

SECRETARY: You are out of order.

SEA: Dreams are real, and reality is less than early morning mist.

SECRETARY: You are out of order.

SEA: Order is out.

SECRETARY: Hysteria.

HAY: This is not like you, Sea. You're level-headed, imperturbable, unflappable.

SEA: You never did see very far, did you?

BEE: And you always agree.

CHAIRMAN: Oh, has a vote already been. . . ?

SEA: I always agree because I don't want to be troubled. I always agree because I want a quiet life.

HAY: Then agree now.

SEA: But now something troubles me more than you.

BEE: There's nothing to be afraid of. Certainly not there.

TREASURER (*testily*): At worst they're no more than an inconvenience.

SEA: They?

TREASURER (*hastily retreating*): You misheard me.

 (SEA *turns to face the audience while speaking to the others*.)

SEA: You've seen exactly what I can see now. People staring at us. And they're real. As real as anything can be in this delirious world. . . . Some rigid. Some fidgeting. One whispering to a neighbour. One fumbling in a bag of toffees. One surreptitiously picking his nose. You want me to agree that they don't exist. But I can't. I can't. I'm sorry if that upsets your carefully contrived arrangements. I really am because it makes me out of step, and being out of step makes one so conspicuous, and I'm never conspicuous if I can help it. But—they—are—there. So what are you going to do about it?

 (*Throughout this speech concerned looks have flashed between the others—except the* CHAIRMAN, *who still blinks myopically baffled. Pause.*)

CHAIRMAN: Well, now. . . .

SECRETARY (*ignoring* CHAIRMAN *and speaking to* SEA): We did not hear you.

CHAIRMAN: Really? (*Louder.*) Well, now.

SEA: I'm telling you. . . .

SECRETARY: We do not hear you.

SEA: That's an old trick. Put me on the same level as Them. But if you equate me with Them, and you admit that I'm here, then. . . .

SECRETARY: Will the Chairman please take a vote.

SEA: You can't believe that if you ignore them they'll go away.

CHAIRMAN: As long as it is in order. . . .

SEA: At least I can't believe that.

CHAIRMAN: If only I could be sure which item. . . .

SEA: Something must be done about them.

SECRETARY (*to* CHAIRMAN): It doesn't matter. We know what we're doing.

SEA: And the preliminary to doing anything is admitting. . . .

CHAIRMAN: As long as someone. . . . All in favour?

ALL EXCEPT SEA: Aye.

SEA: I've always tried to get along with you.

CHAIRMAN: Against?

SEA: But I can't accept. . . .

CHAIRMAN: Carried.

　　(SEA *gets up, goes to the audience and stares at them.*)

SECRETARY: Nem con.

SEA: You are, aren't you? There, I mean. Not figments of a disordered imagination. How could you be? I've no imagination. Never had.

TREASURER: The fool!

SECRETARY: At which point Sea left the meeting.

SEA (*swinging round*): I heard that. Written off. Very clever. From now on I don't count—if I ever did. But it doesn't solve anything. Because I'm going to join Them. And if I can join Them. . . . Work the rest out for yourselves.

　　(SEA *hurries out. The relief of the other committee members is patent, and in the case of the* SECRETARY, *audible.*)

TREASURER: For a moment it seemed as though a crisis. . . .

SECRETARY: It's past.

CHAIRMAN: Of course it is. All for, none against. We may have our little. . . . But when it comes to a vote we all. . . . What now?

SECRETARY: Any other business?

HAY: We'll be finished early with any luck.

CHAIRMAN: Is there any. . . ?

BEE: If I might. . . .

HAY: Luck!

BEE: Propose a vote of thanks to our Secretary.

SECRETARY: It's not necessary.

BEE: For extricating us from the recent unfortunate situation.

SECRETARY: There was no situation.

BEE: Was there not?

SECRETARY: No.

BEE: I thought. . . .

SECRETARY: There was no situation at all.

BEE: But there might have been.

SECRETARY: There might have been, but there wasn't.

BEE: If I might say so. . . .

SECRETARY: I'd rather you didn't.

BEE: That was entirely due to quick thinking and thorough knowledge of procedure at meetings.

SECRETARY: The Chartered Institute of Secretaries noted my capabilities when I passed their final examination. There's no need to labour the point.

BEE: I still say a crisis was averted.

SECRETARY: There was no crisis. Therefore it was not averted.

HAY: I'm quite willing to second a vote of thanks.

SECRETARY: A vote of thanks assumes a crisis. A crisis assumes the existence of something which we have agreed not to mention.

TREASURER: Which does not exist.

SECRETARY: As the Treasurer remarks—which does not exist.

(*A* MEMBER OF THE AUDIENCE *climbs on to the stage, and sits in* SEA's *vacant seat. There is a long pause.*)

CHAIRMAN: As you were saying. . . .

SECRETARY: Which does not exist.

(*The* MEMBER OF THE AUDIENCE *is perfectly at ease. If a woman she might take out her knitting.*)

BEE: On the other hand I have always found a vote of thanks acceptable.

(BEE *finds it difficult not to give little sidelong glances at the* MEMBER OF THE AUDIENCE. *Particularly as that person is now vigorously searching through shopping bag or pockets.*)

BEE: A vote of thanks does a lot to oil the administrative wheels. It is—to coin a phrase—twice-blessed: it blesses the ones who give, and the one who receives, warming the cockles of all our hearts.

(*The* MEMBER OF THE AUDIENCE *produces a large and crinkly paper bag containing sweets, and makes a considerable noise getting a sweet out, shaking it to get at a particular sweet.*)

BEE: Moreover a vote of thanks costs nothing. Many's the occasion when a vote of thanks has avoided a more costly recognition of services—such as a gold watch or a statue in a public place. Personally I am always prepared to accept. . . .

(*The* MEMBER OF THE AUDIENCE *thrusts the bag under his nose.*)

BEE (*feebly*): A vote of thanks.

(*Flops back into seat.*)

HAY: Some—things—are difficult—to—ignore.

SECRETARY: Some things are not spoken of.

TREASURER: We have agreed that there is no problem, but. . . .

SECRETARY: Given time any problem will solve itself.

TREASURER: But how?

SECRETARY: That is not our concern.

TREASURER: I meant—speaking hypothetically of course—what would be our position after the problem has solved itself? An example. Here is a mouse. Here is a piece of cheese.

CHAIRMAN: I beg your. . . .

TREASURER (*loudly and clearly*): Here is a mouse. Here is a piece of cheese.

CHAIRMAN (*blinking at thin air*): I really must get new glasses.

TREASURER: The cheese is in a trap. Problem: how does the mouse get the cheese? It waits for the problem to solve itself. The trap makes no move. After waiting long enough the mouse nibbles at the cheese. Bang! (*Claps hands.*)

HAY: Please! I can't stand sudden reports.

TREASURER: For the mouse there is no longer any problem.

SECRETARY: If your mouse had ignored the cheese from the beginning, there would never have been any problem.

CHAIRMAN: I confess I have some difficulty in following. . . . I understood that Hay was about to. . . . A vote. . . .

HAY: I second. That is if you don't consider such a vote premature while. . . .

(*Starts to point at the* MEMBER OF THE AUDIENCE, *but remembers that such people are not supposed to exist.*)

HAY: While that—vacant seat. . . .

(*The* MEMBER OF THE AUDIENCE *blows nose vigorously.*)

BEE: I heard nothing.

HAY: However I am delighted to congratulate the Secretary, whose policy of masterly inactivity is an inspiration to us all. I only wish I could ignore—nothing—with equal coolness.

(*The* MEMBER OF THE AUDIENCE *discovers an empty paper bag.* HAY *watches fascinated as the* MEMBER OF THE AUDIENCE *blows up the bag.*)

HAY: Though I must confess I experience personal difficulty in disregarding the lack of activity which is not taking place opposite. And I warn the Secretary that I cannot stand sudden explosions even when they are caused by a paper bag that does not exist.

(*The* MEMBER OF THE AUDIENCE *contemplates the blown-up bag.*)

HAY: You're nearer than I am. Stop it.

SECRETARY: How can I stop anything that isn't there?
   (BEE *suddenly puts fingers in ears*.)
SECRETARY: What do you think you're doing?
   (*The* MEMBER OF THE AUDIENCE *raises a hand*.)
HAY: I can't. . . . I can't!
   (*Turns and runs. The* MEMBER OF THE AUDIENCE *hits the bag*.)
BEE: I didn't hear it. I didn't hear it.
   (*Chuckling, the* MEMBER OF THE AUDIENCE *stows away the torn bag*.)
BEE: But Hay may be in need of. . . . A little pity is worth a deal of help.
   (*Hurries away after* HAY. *The* MEMBER OF THE AUDIENCE *sits back and chuckles at the memory of the bang*.)
SECRETARY: Sheer lack of moral fibre.
TREASURER: Congratulations. You didn't even blink.
SECRETARY: At what?
MEMBER OF THE AUDIENCE: (*Chuckles*.)
TREASURER: I admire the stiffness of your upper lip.
CHAIRMAN: I can't help wondering whether. . . .
SECRETARY: Hold on. That's all that's necessary.
CHAIRMAN: Most reassuring, but are there enough of us to. . . ?
SECRETARY: Grit your teeth and cling to your convictions.
MEMBER OF THE AUDIENCE: (*Chuckles*.)
SECRETARY: There's no one here but us three.
MEMBER OF THE AUDIENCE: (*Chuckles*.)
CHAIRMAN: Exactly. The rules. . . .
TREASURER: You mean—have we a quorum?
MEMBER OF THE AUDIENCE: (*Chuckles*.)
SECRETARY: There was no more business.
TREASURER: The vote of thanks. . . .
SECRETARY: It can wait.
CHAIRMAN: I had prepared a closing. . . . A few well-chosen. . . .
SECRETARY: It can wait.
   (*Two more members of the audience climb on to the stage and take the seats vacated by* HAY *and* BEE.)
CHAIRMAN: Ah, there you are.
   (*The* TREASURER *and the* SECRETARY *look at each other*.)
SECRETARY: There's no problem if you refuse to admit it.
   (*In silence the* TREASURER *gets up and leaves*.)
SECRETARY: There is no problem.
   (*Three more members of the audience climb on to the stage. One sits in the* TREASURER's *seat*.)
SECRETARY: What is not admitted doesn't have to be faced.
   (*The* SECRETARY *follows the* TREASURER. *A member of the*

audience sits in the SECRETARY's *place. The remaining new-comer stands by the* CHAIRMAN, *waiting. As the* CHAIRMAN *stands to deliver the closing remarks, the newcomer sits on the vacated chair.*)

CHAIRMAN: As we are all. . . . I thought this a suitable occasion for. . . . But first I should like to. . . . As you are all quite aware. . . . Not that I have any intentions. . . . But to congratulate all concerned on the solid. . . . I stand here. Confident. And in any case. What has been begun. . . . Thank you.

(*The* CHAIRMAN *is about to be reseated, but there is no seat left.*)

CHAIRMAN: Oh, really? I was under the impression that. . . . I may have been. . . . In which case. . . .

(*The* CHAIRMAN *walks away, but at the last moment turns as though to address the group around the table.*)

CHAIRMAN: No. Impossible. Of course, impossible.

(*Goes out leaving the new group in possession.*)*

Unit 13

The Director

The planning and presentation of a play is controlled by the director or producer (the terms are synonymous). He must decide on the overall style of the production, its visual impact and meaning. What he sees in his imagination has to be translated into action on a stage. He will conduct rehearsals at which the moves, exits, entrances and so on are practised and the actors and actresses guided towards the full realisation of their roles and an understanding of their relationships to other characters. It was only in the late nineteenth century that the job of director was particularly identified. In earlier times the organisation was generally in the hands of the leading actor (called an actor manager) who arranged the production to show off his own individual gifts. There is a particularly vivid description of Mr Crummles, an actor manager in Charles Dickens's *Nicholas Nickleby*.

It is obvious that the job of a director is complex and demanding. Our description is only a simplified summary. The bibliography contains further information. There is a considerable range of opinion concerning the way a director should work. He may have rigid and minutely detailed plans for every movement to be made: Meyerhold (1874–1943) who, at one time, was associated with Stanislavsky, worked like this, whereas Brecht (1898–1956) allowed every movement to evolve during rehearsals. Eric Bentley, who worked with Brecht and translated most of his plays into English, describes how he attended a rehearsal which appeared so casual that he was still waiting for it to 'start' when it ended!

Most directors would agree that some general plan for the production is desirable. A simple means of achieving this is to make a 'prompt copy' by interleaving the text with plain pages divided into columns. Everything that is to happen in movement, sound and light (or even the closing of the curtain-tabs) is marked opposite the appropriate part of the script. Each new happening is called a 'cue' and cues are numbered.

In order to fix stage positions, the acting area is divided into sections. The diagram shows the positions on a conventional proscenium stage—remember that, as an actor, Stage Right is *your* right as you face the audience.

Up Right		Up Centre		Up Left
	Up Right of Centre		Up Left of Centre	
Stage Right	Right of Centre	Centre	Left of Centre	Stage Left
	Down Right of Centre		Down Left of Centre	
Down Right		Down Centre		Down Left

AUDIENCE

Deciding moves for the characters before the rehearsals start often takes place in the quiet of the producer's study. He meets his actors with what Rodney Wood (formerly artistic director of the Scarborough Theatre) once described as 'a basis for negotiation'. At rehearsals rearrangements or alterations may occur as the actors work on the suggestions: the process of fixing positions is known as 'blocking'.

Now here is an extract from a prompt copy. Study it carefully.

DISCUSSION AND ACTIVITY

1. Notice the small sketch of the stage; words underlined are the exact moment when a cue is to take place.
2. Make a prompt copy for the opening scene of a play of

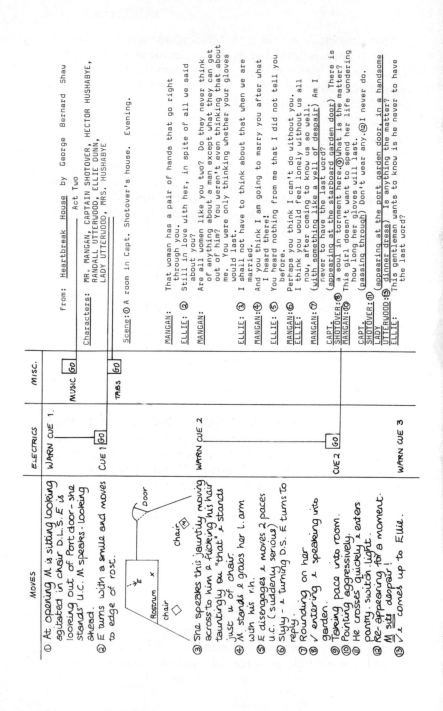

MOVES	ELECTRICS	MISC.	

MOVES

① At opening M is sitting looking agitated in chair D.L.S. E is looking out of Port door - she stands? U.C. M speaks - looking ahead.

② E turns with a smile and moves to edge of rost.

(diagram: chair ◇, Rostrum x, E →, chair ⊗, Door)

③ She speaks this jauntily moving across to him & flicking his hair tauntingly on "that" & stands just U of chair.

④ M stands & grabs her L. arm with his r.h.

⑤ E disengages & moves 2 paces U.C. (suddenly serious)

⑥ Slyly - & turning D.S. E turns to reply.

⑦ Rounding on her.

⑧ V entering & speaking into garden.

⑨ Taking pace into room.

⑩ Pointing aggressively.

⑪ He crosses quickly & enters pantry. switch light.

⑫ Re-appearing for a moment. M still deeper!

⑬ V & comes up to Ellie.

ELECTRICS

WARN CUE 1.
CUE 1 [Go]
WARN CUE 2
CUE 2 [Go]
WARN CUE 3

MISC.

MUSIC [Go]
TABS [Go]

---

from: Heartbreak House by George Bernard Shaw

Act Two

Characters: MR. MANGAN, CAPTAIN SHOTOVER, HECTOR HUSHABYE, RANDALL UTTERWOOD, ELLIE DUNN, LADY UTTERWOOD, MRS. HUSHABYE

Scene: ① A room in Capt. Shotover's house. Evening.

MANGAN: That woman has a pair of hands that go right through you.

ELLIE: ② Still in love with her, in spite of all we said about you?

MANGAN: Are all women like you two? Do they never think of anything about a man except what they can get out of him? You weren't even thinking that about me. You were only thinking whether your gloves would last.

ELLIE: ③ I shall not have to think about that when we are married.

MANGAN: ④ And think I am going to marry you after what I heard there!

ELLIE: ⑤ You heard nothing from me that I did not tell you before.

MANGAN: ⑥ Perhaps you think I can't do without you.

ELLIE: I think you would feel lonely without us all now, after coming to know us so well.

MANGAN: ⑦ (with something like a yell of despair) Am I never to have the last word?

CAPT. SHOTOVER: ⑧ (appearing at the starboard garden door) There is a soul in torment here. ⑨ What is the matter?

MANGAN: ⑩ This girl doesn't want to spend her life wondering how long her gloves will last.

CAPT. SHOTOVER: ⑪ (passing through) Don't wear any. ⑫ I never do.

LADY UTTERWOOD: ⑬ (appearing at the port garden door, in a handsome dinner dress) Is anything the matter?

ELLIE: This gentleman wants to know is he never to have the last word?

your choice. You will find that this involves decisions about the staging and style before you can start.

3. Look at Stanislavsky's production notes for *Othello* in *Creating a Role*.

4. How can improvisation be blended with firm direction?

5. A story is told that Joan Littlewood, the controversial director of Theatre Workshop, went on stage half an hour before a performance was due to start and moved all the furniture round. Why do you think she did this? what might it have achieved?

6. The director/producer is a recent development: research into the emergence of this specialist branch of theatre and decide on the advantages of modern practice. Should a director ever take part as an actor?

BIBLIOGRAPHY

James Roose Evans: *Directing a Play*, Studio Vista, London, 1968.
(A most stimulating discussion of the producer's task.)
John Fernald: *Sense of Direction*, Secker & Warburg, London, 1968.
The Oxford Companion to the Theatre, OUP, 1967 edition.
(See the article 'Producer'.)
K. S. Stanislavsky: *Creating a Role*, Penguin, Harmondsworth, 1963.

Unit 14

The Stage Manager

No attempt has been made so far to differentiate between amateur and professional performances but, unfortunately, the distinction is never more marked than in the area of stage management. Any director will tell you that to have a good stage manager is to be half-way to an effective production.

The S.M. (the common abbreviation) is involved in the planning from the earliest stages. It is his task to convert the ideas of the producer and designer into practical realities. He has his own prompt copy which enables him to record every detail of the production as it evolves. Moves, cues, scene changes and calls are all noted and from this you will see that the S.M. is in a position to conduct a rehearsal in the director's absence.

Study the following list of an S.M.'s duties:

1. To be responsible for the discipline of the cast on and off stage (this includes arranging calls and ensuring that everyone is available at the correct time).
2. To control all practical details of a production (excluding Front of House duties).
3. To make scaled plans from the designer's drawings.
4. To ensure that all scenery, props, etc. are constructed and in position at the required time.
5. To liaise with lighting and sound technicians to ensure correct cueing.

You will see that 2 really covers all the rest. Once the dress-rehearsal is over the director has no further task but to sit in the audience and learn from his experience. He may wish to make a few points or alter something which appears faulty but, generally, a good director will restrict his activities to informal discussion and encouragement whilst the complete responsibility lies with the S.M.

Look now at Fig. 10 which shows an S.M.'s first plan for the design by Susan ffitch described in Unit 10. Subsequent plans would give the exact dimensions of the pieces of scenery and individual flats (canvas-covered wooden frames). These would be numbered P.1., O.P.1 etc. 'P' stands for Prompt side which is traditionally Stage Left and 'O.P.' stands for Opposite Prompt side. (Mr Crummles often used these terms.)

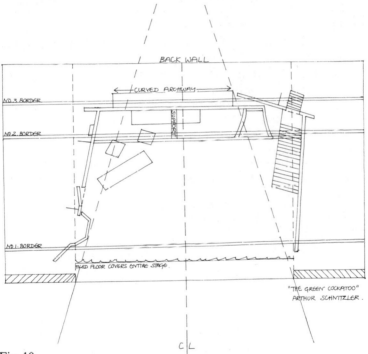

Fig. 10

It takes a great deal of experience and expertise to become an efficient and imaginative stage manager. The skills are gained by a combination of practical experience and careful research. The S.M. may begin in very simple ways, by organising straightforward productions of short scenes or helping more experienced exponents. Efficient handling must be established as a method right from the start. The S.M. must also use his skill and imagination in solving problems set by the director and designer. He should avoid a negative approach.

Practice in stage management can be acquired by electing an S.M. in your improvisations and acted scenes.

It is useful to keep a notebook of hints and ideas. Several books on stage management and related activities will give valuable advice. Collect ideas for stage management, scenery construction and planning that are appropriate for your studio, hall or theatre.

Further discussion and activity
1. Looking at the plan, decide on the nature and purpose of sight lines.
2. Make a scale plan for your design in Unit 10—squared graph paper is very helpful.
3. Refer to any book on stage management and learn how to construct a flat.

BIBLIOGRAPHY

P. Goffin: *The Art and Science of Stage Management*, Garnet Miller, London, 1953.
P. Corry: *Amateur Theatrecraft*, Museum Press, London, 1961.
Hendrik Baker: *Stage Management and Theatrecraft*, Garnet Miller, London, 1969.

Unit 15

Documentary Drama

A great number of plays in Western world drama deal with actual historical events and people; recent insights into life inside China suggest that this tendency is also emerging in the East.

We have already encountered Osborne's *Luther*, Robert Bolt's *A Man for all Seasons* and T. S. Eliot's *Murder in the Cathedral*; a comprehensive list would include, for example, Shakespeare's History plays, Marlowe's *Edward the Second*, John Ford's *Perkin Warbeck* and Gordon Daviot's *Richard of Bordeaux*.

The question to be asked is how accurately the playwright must observe historical facts in so far as they are known. It is frequently difficult to ascertain the truth concerning contemporary happenings. It is much more complicated when distant historical events are being used. But this is not the end of the problems. Some playwrights deliberately distort or alter the facts to suit their particular intention. For example the well-known figure of Joan of Arc appears as 'La Pucelle' in Shakespeare's *Henry VI* Part I. Driving English soldiers before her she exudes demoniac power and by Act v scene 4 when she is finally captured and derided her witchcraft seems confirmed. Joan is shown being burned as a witch in Bernard Shaw's play *St Joan*, but in an earlier version by Schiller, *The Maid of Orleans* (1801), she is shown dying heroically on the battlefield.

Rolf Hochhuth, whose play *Soldiers* seemed to make some unsavoury and fictitious allegations against Winston Churchill, the wartime leader, comments:

I do not think that the author of historical plays is entitled to invent vital incidents. In fact, I think that in doing so he would ruin himself artistically. For example in *The Maid of Orleans* Schiller made Joan die a heroic death on the battlefield instead of showing her real end at the stake, Shaw stuck to the facts and I find his ending infinitely more moving.

George Bernard Shaw's *St Joan* (1924) was first played by Dame Sybil Thorndike and remains one of the greatest virtuoso roles for an actress. It is a compassionate and yet unsentimental account which contrasts sharply with Shakespeare's hysterical and prejudiced treatment. It was inevitable that a French play on the same theme would appear. Jean Anouilh's *The Lark* was first seen by British audiences in 1955 in translation by the English playwright Christopher Fry. In a series of flashbacks at her trial Joan herself conducts us through the events and influences in her life. The ending is unexpected and the unusual structure of the play brings to this story, which Hermon Ould also used for his *Joan the Maid* (1920), a freshness and vitality which could so easily have been lacking. The over-romantic *Maid of Orleans* by Schiller gave Bertold Brecht the starting-point for his *Joan of the Stockyards*. But the scene is changed from France to the Chicago of Al Capone and Joan works as a 'Black Straw Hat' (the equivalent of the Salvation Army).

These five versions of the same historical person and the events in her life show us how dangerous it is to assume that we are seeing historical truth when we watch a play. It has already been stressed how difficult it is to achieve truth and accuracy.

A play by Royce Ryton about the abdication of King Edward VIII was sent to Buckingham Palace for scrutiny in April 1972. It was returned with a letter from the Queen's secretary:

I write to thank you for your letter of April 7th and for the copy of your play entitled *Crown Matrimonial*. Your courtesy in sending the manuscript for any observations is appreciated but I am to say this is not a matter upon which it is desired to comment.

Attempts to present a truthful yet vivid picture are exemplified by 'documentary drama' which is based on primary sources, i.e. original manuscripts, letters, photos, maps, eyewitness reports etc. The Victoria Theatre at Stoke-on-Trent has been particularly successful with this type of drama and it is now being undertaken by an increasingly large number of companies. The form of presentation may be straightforwardly realistic or alternatively offered in a comic or music hall style. Joan Littlewood's production of *Oh What a Lovely War!* has an illuminated sign on stage showing the enormous casualty figures of World War I, with terse official comments, but the actors adopt the characters of performers in a pierrot show on a seaside pier.

Documentary drama makes very free use of many different theatrical styles. It does not feel bound by the usual play-writing conventions. Films, posters, music, political speeches may all be included in a single performance. There are dangers in the multiplicity, but it offers the possibility of exciting and relevant theatre.

In an attempt to define 'documentary theatre' Peter Weiss, best known for his play the *Marat/Sade*, has written:

Documentary Theatre refrains from all invention: it takes authentic material and puts it on the stage, unaltered in content, edited in form. . . . Documentary Theatre is a reflection of life as we witness it through the mass media, re-defined by asking various critical questions . . . it must gain entrance to factories, schools, sports grounds, meeting halls.

From *Theatre Quarterly*, I, 1

The following article from the *Daily Telegraph* draws attention to the dangers of documentary drama. In all fairness, one should say that it is often an honest attempt to make drama relevant to people who may find the problems of kings and saints somewhat unreal!

The Belgrade Theatre, Coventry, has done good work before. Presumably it will do so again. Meanwhile it is not doing itself much good with a show called *You Must be Joking!*

It is doing no good whatever to the cause vaguely known as documentary theatre—the urge which periodically erupts at reps to work up a show which they can call their own from local life and local history.

Always a temptingly facile form of entertainment with its songs and slides and other Brechtiana based upon a bit of 'research', it reaches rock bottom to my mind with this long, slow meandering account of Coventry's motor industry since the 1890s.

It would be hard to conceive of a less imaginative approach to an often turbulent and exciting story of human enterprise, injustice, strife and stolidity.

True we get a glimpse in mime of the monotony of work in a motor car factory. And of the miseries of unemployment over the years and the exploitation of worker by boss, no doubt is left at all.

But this is all familiar stuff for theatre audiences. It needs reminding, real writing and a creative imagination which would place the facts in an arresting light.

Neither Christopher Honer as director nor David Holman as writer has organised this episodic history with enough dramatic fancy to give it theatrical continuity. They haven't even bothered to drain the worker-boss dialogue of the jargon which infests all such relations, nor have they found any humour in it.

And for music they have chosen a small folk group whose songs, though bearing enough on the theme, are murmured in an idiom (mainly to guitars) which robs the show of any possible sense of period.

Stuck on the right of the stage, these rather dreary musicians have also to contend with a lethargic production which must be in its own way making history in the art of unpregnant pauses.

DISCUSSION AND ACTIVITY

1. Use the Jackdaw File *Joan of Arc* as the basis for your own play about St Joan and compare your product with various plays outlined in this unit. Look particularly at the various speeches Joan makes in her defence.

2. Read and act scenes from Alan Pater's *Close the Coal House Door* and Charles Chiltern's *Oh What a Lovely War!*
3. Devise a play *The Rise and Fall of the Beatles* using all available sources.
4. Select an event that created great interest in your district and research into the details connected with it; then make a play.

BIBLIOGRAPHY

Brian Clark: *Group Theatre*, Pitman, London, 1971.
(Chapter 6 deals with the group approach to documentary.)
Martin Esslin: *Brief Chronicles*, Temple Smith, London, 1970.
(The chapter 'Truth and Documentation'.)
Theatre Quarterly, I, 1, 1971.

Brecht and a History Play?

In the *Daily Telegraph* article which you read in Unit 15 the writer uses the term 'Brechtiana'. As one of the aims of this book is to enable you to visit the theatre and read criticism with a sharpened awareness, this expression of the writer's own invention must be explained. But more than this the influence of Brecht in modern theatre has been profound and thus we should examine some of the details.

Brecht's play *Mother Courage and her Children* deals with some events in the Thirty Years War which ravaged Europe between the years 1618 and 1648. The slaughter was horrific and the suffering intense: huge armies swayed across the continent living off the land; on many occasions the peasant people had no idea of the issues involved or whose side they were on.

Standard histories of the Thirty Years War, while conveying much of this information, usually present the events in the terms of the military leaders: Tilly, Wallenstein and Gustavus Adolphus and, although the war may strike us as having been a particularly futile Protestant/Catholic struggle, the lasting impression is of a series of victories and defeats.

Brecht's play gives a totally different picture. Mother Courage hauls her canteen wagon across Europe supplying soldiers on either side. She loses all her children in the war but is sustained by her wily and wiry energy and the sheer need for survival. Events like the death of Tilly and Gustavus Adolphus have little relevance for Mother Courage—during Tilly's funeral she makes an inventory of supplies:

CHAPLAIN: The funeral is just starting out.

MOTHER COURAGE: Pity about the Chief—twenty-two pairs of socks—getting killed that way. They say it was an accident. There was fog over the fields that morning and the fog was to blame. The Chief called up another regiment, told 'em to fight to the death, rode back again, missed his way in the fog, went forward instead of back and ran smack into a bullet in the thick of the battle—only four lanterns left.

MOTHER COURAGE: Seventeen leather belts. . . . Then you don't think the war might end?

CHAPLAIN: Because a commander's dead? Don't be childish, they're sixpence a dozen. There are always heroes.

(from scene 6)

Scene 8 is entitled: '1632. In this same year Gustavus Adolphus fell in the battle of Lutzen. The peace threatens Mother Courage with ruin. Her brave son performs one heroic deed too many and comes to a shameful end.'

[Some peasants attempt to sell bedding to Mother Courage.]

MOTHER COURAGE (*from inside the wagon*): Must you come at crack of dawn?

YOUNG MAN: We've been walking all night, twenty miles it was, we have to be back today.

MOTHER COURAGE: What do I want with bed feathers? People don't even have houses.

YOUNG MAN: At least wait until you see them.

OLD WOMAN: Nothing doing here either, let's go—

YOUNG MAN: And let 'em sign away the roof over our heads for taxes? Maybe she'll pay three guilders if you throw in that bracelet. (*Bells start ringing.*) You hear Mother?

VOICE: It's peace! The King of Sweden has been killed!

MOTHER COURAGE (*sticks her head out of the wagon—she hasn't done her hair yet*): Bells! What are bells for in the middle of the week?

CHAPLAIN (*crawling from under the wagon*): What's that there shouting?

YOUNG MAN: It's peace.

CHAPLAIN: Peace!

MOTHER COURAGE: Don't tell me peace has broken out—when I've just gone and brought all these supplies!

We are confronted with a series of scenes each, like scene 8, introduced by a headline-like statement: in the theatre these may be projected on to the cyclorama, spoken by a 'neutral' voice or appear as a newspaper placard. The war has already started as the play begins and continues after the final scene; there is no satisfying resolution. Events are sometimes separated by an interval of years and the action, sometimes totally realistic, sometimes both funny and horrific, is punctuated by songs. Our last impression is of the soldiers singing:

> Dangers, surprises, devastations—
> The war takes hold and will not quit.
> But though it last three generations
> We shall get nothing out of it.
> Starvation, filth and cold enslave us
> The army robs us of our pay.
> Only a miracle can save us
> And miracles have had their day.
> Christians Awake! The winter's gone!
> The snows depart. The dead sleep on.
> And though you may not long survive
> Get out of bed and look alive!

The effect of the unusual structure of the play and the mixture of music hall stylisation and realism is to prevent our total emotional involvement in the play as a whole; although at any one moment, such as the death of Katrin, we may be completely transfixed. Rather we are able to form some opinion about the situations and consider their implications for us.

In training his actors Brecht insisted that they, too, should not become so involved in the lives of the characters they were presenting that they were unable to think objectively about them. He frequently asked them to rehearse scenes of dialogue in reported speech suggesting that the actors were more like the onlookers at an accident giving an eye-witness account rather than like the victims themselves. This, of course, represents a revolution against the ideas pioneered by Stanislavsky—an example of the non-static nature of the art of theatre.

Brecht nevertheless focused attention carefully; it is

therefore no contradiction that he insisted on absolute realism in costume and properties so that no inconsistencies should mar the individual incidents being considered. There was no attempt to delude the audience that they were not in a theatre—no curtain opened, the lighting equipment was fully visible and there was a workshop atmosphere about the productions. The ingredients of Brechtiana are now easier for you to identify. There is no doubt that they have revitalised production methods, but at their worst they can degenerate into gimmickry and slipshod practice.

Although Brecht wrote *Mother Courage* in 1938–9 after fleeing the Nazi regime in Germany it is his post-war

Plate VII   *Courtesy, Hainer Hill*

production with The Berliner Ensemble in East Berlin which is usually considered to be a theatrical landmark today. The playwright's wife Helen Weigel took the part of Mother Courage and her performance was so memorable that detailed studies of her every action and expression have been preserved in photographic and written form.

It was Joan Littlewood who first produced *Mother Courage* in England and it is hardly surprising that her Theatre Workshop later devised the drama about the 1914–18 War: *Oh What a Lovely War!* This subsequently filmed play relied heavily on Brechtian techniques and like *Mother Courage* was able to comment on war in general against the background of a specific and similarly wasteful catastrophe.

DISCUSSION AND ACTIVITY

1. Obtain copies of *Mother Courage* (in Methuen paperback) and work on some scenes.
2. Compare this play with *The Long and the Short and the Tall, Then*, R. C. Sherrif's *Journey's End* and *US* (of which there is a detailed account in D. Adland's *Group Approach to Drama, Book 6*).
3. All these plays contain some protest or comment on the horror and degradation of war. The poems of Siegfried Sassoon, Wilfred Owen and Edward Thomas, Benjamin

Britten's *War Requiem* and Robert Graves's autobiography *Goodbye to All That* and Bob Dylan's protest songs are all equally vigorous in their condemnation of the waste and destruction of human life. How influential are these protests? Discuss the effectiveness of plays, songs and poems in voicing political or religious opinions or in making protests.

4. Several composers have written music for *Mother Courage*—the most recent being the English composer Alan Ridout (1972). Try writing your own music for the song included in this unit.

5. Involve a member of your history department in a debate on the value of *Mother Courage* as a documentary or history of the Thirty Years War.

6. It is almost impossible to remain objective in a discussion of war; the writing of this unit was completed on the eve of Remembrance Sunday. Do you detect any value judgements that are unacceptable? Are any of the plays discussed here dramatised propaganda?

BIBLIOGRAPHY

C. V. Wedgewood: *The Thirty Years War*, Penguin, Harmondsworth, 1937.

Arthur Marwick: *War and Society in the Twentieth Century*, Open Univ. Press, 1973.

Also see material contained in the Nuffield Humanities Project.

Unit 17

Television:
Techniques of Production

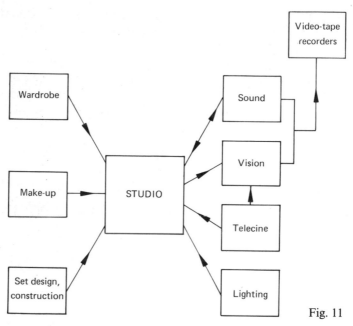

Fig. 11

The aim of this unit is to present some of the basic techniques of television production and by the end of it you should be able to work out, with reasonable accuracy, the techniques employed in television programmes that you watch. If you look at the controls of a domestic television receiver you will see that it is designed to receive two sets of signals—vision and sound. This may appear obvious, but with a little thought you will see that the whole of production techniques must be directly related to these two basic elements. Figure 11 is a diagrammatic representation of the way in which a television studio functions. Divide the elements of the system between vision and sound.

Some of the technical details will by now be familiar to you—for example set design, construction, costume, lighting and make-up. Much of the support system for a stage production is relevant to television.

Vision

The television camera　The television camera can reproduce electronically images 'read' by the lens system. The lens control is similar to that of the film cine-camera and the control of light falling on the sensitive tube of the television camera by variation of the size of the aperture is essentially the same. The camera can have either a series of lenses housed in a turret, a fixed-angle lens, or a 'zoom' lens.

A turret houses three or four lenses which have different angles, and can be rotated. (Fig. 12.)

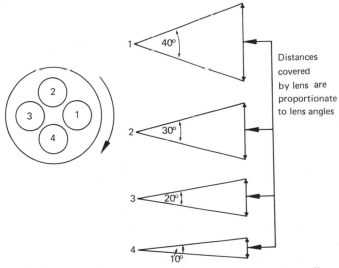

Fig. 12: 1. Very wide angle: long shot　3. Normal angle: medium shot
　　　　2. Wide angle: long shot　　　4. Narrow angle: close-up

In this way the angle of vision can be selected to suit the shot required by the director.

Another popular system of lens control is the zoom lens, which the camera-man can move between those angles mentioned above. The nature of the extent of the zoom is normally shown as a ratio, such as 4:1 or 10:1. This refers to the ratio of the extremes of the lens's range.

Either lens system can be used to achieve the basic series of shots. These are shown in Fig. 13.

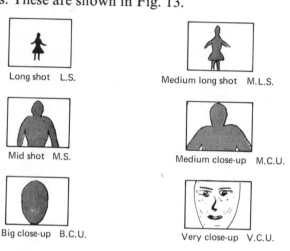

Long shot   L.S.

Medium long shot   M.L.S.

Mid shot   M.S.

Medium close-up   M.C.U.

Big close-up   B.C.U.

Very close-up   V.C.U.

Extreme close-up   E.C.U.

Fig. 13

The zoom lens moved 'on shot' can have an interesting focusing effect for the viewer. It is also useful for moving from a general shot (wide angle, sometimes called a context shot) to a specific area to be scrutinised (in close-up) in situations which demand flexible coverage. A football match is one good example of this technique; can you think of others?

Television cameras have one very important advantage over cine-cameras. They work synchronised with each other. This means that many of the effects in scene changing laboriously produced by the physical cutting and welding of cine-film can be obtained immediately and directly by the director of the programme, giving him greater control over his visual material. In the cinema this work is carried out by the editor in the cutting room.

We have concentrated so far on the control of light falling on the camera. As we can move the camera either by a crane system or by a counter-weighted dolly this gives it greater power to represent in an interesting way what it 'sees'. The camera is usually mounted on a movable stand called a dolly and this permits its movement forwards and backwards (tracking) or from side to side (crabbing). At the same time the camera height can be easily and quickly adjusted.

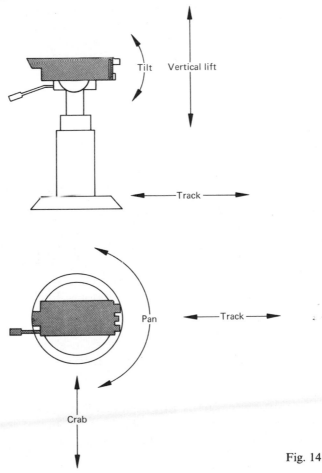

Fig. 14

It is also possible to move the camera on its mount either in a lateral circular way (panning) or vertically about an axis (tilting).

All these moves can be made with variations of pace and in conjunction with one another. The director is responsible for picking angles and movements to suit the mood of the subject.

Types of visual image

Caption   A caption is any visual material which is mounted in a static two-dimensional way—this includes pictures, maps, diagrams, titles, credits etc. Normally caption material is handled by the graphics department and is mounted on card (often black) in the ratio 4:3, the ratio of the oblong television screen.

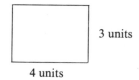

3 units

4 units

At its simplest the caption sequence may be words on a black background which name the programme's participants. Each card in the sequence has perhaps one or two names written on it.

Camera 1 takes in captions numbered 1, 3, 5 and 7 in the sequence: Camera 2 takes in captions 2, 4 and 6. By switching between cameras 1 and 2 the director can obtain a consecutive sequence of six caption changes. Each time that he switches from camera 1 to 2 or 2 to 1 then the used caption card is removed by an operator known as a caption 'puller'. This sounds simple but it is quite a tense and tricky job— think how often you have seen captional material moved before it is 'off-shot'.

Live material   Really this includes live material normally shot in the studio involving 'live' action, but of course it is extended to include live material shot, say, during an outside broadcast.

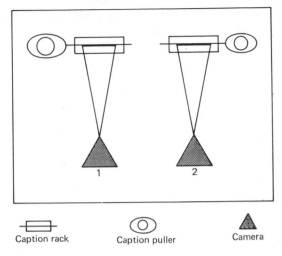

Caption rack   Caption puller   Camera

Figure 15 Setting for a two-camera caption sequence

Telecine   It is possible to shoot parts of television programmes out on location on 16 mm film and then insert
film 'clips' into the studio production. Usually the telecine
department is centralised and is 'timed in' or 'cued' into
a programme by the production control staff. An obvious
example of a complex mixture of telecine and 'live' images
is a news bulletin. Recent developments in television include
shooting outside scenes on to videotape rather than going
through a conversion from 16 mm film to tape.

This in very simple terms describes the operation of the
visual side of a production. The other element is sound.

Sound

Sound may come from several different sources. It may be
an input from microphones, tapes or discs. It may well be a
mixture of all three. Look at the demands of the following
situation, the opening of a serial episode.

(i)   Signature tune (for captions—from disc)
(ii) Mix in road menders (natural sound from tape)
(iii) Mix in actors (microphones).

There are several types of microphone:

1. *Directional microphone*   often used where the presence

of a microphone is not obtrusive, as, for example, in an interview situation.

2. *Small microphone*   either slung round the neck or clipped to the individual's clothing. This is linked to the sound recording system by a wire.

3. *Boom microphone*   this microphone is slung on the end of a pole over the top of people to be recorded. It is normally used in dramatic presentations as it can accommodate more than one person at a time and does not interfere with the movement of the actors.

4. *Radio-microphone*   this is similar to the neck or clip microphone, but is connected to a small radio transmitter carried unobtrusively by the presenter. This method is mainly used by those performers who do not want to be hampered by a microphone cable running 'off-set'. It is generally acknowledged that the performance characteristics of such a device are less satisfactory than the other methods outlined. However, there have been some major improvements in design recently.

5. *Hand-microphone*   this type of microphone is held and used in those situations where there is little movement and no desire to conceal the sound recording facility.

Voice-over   This technique is used by a presenter who talks 'over' a clip of film, describing the contents. An example of this is the frequent use of 'voice-over' in presenting news.

DISCUSSION AND ACTIVITY

This unit has attempted to define in a fairly simple way the techniques that directly influence those signals which are transmitted to a domestic television receiver. Prepare a tabulated sheet as shown. Watch a television programme individually or in a group and tick as many techniques as possible that you recognise. Look at the results. How much about the programme's nature and content does your survey tell you? Was the programme satisfactory?

TECHNIQUE OR DEVICE	DEFINITION

CAPTIONS

(A) CAMERA SHOTS:
    Long Shot
    Medium Long Shot
    Mid. Shot
    Medium Close-up
    Big Close-up
    Very Close-up
    Extreme Close-up
    Zoom

(B) CAMERA MOVEMENT:
    Tilting
    Panning
    Tracking
    Crabbing

TYPES OF SOUND:
    Music
    Natural sound
    Voice
    Voice over film

TYPES OF MICROPHONE:
    Boom
    Clip
    Stand
    Radio Microphone

Unit 18

The Programme in Production

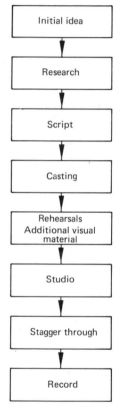

Fig. 15

This diagram traces the progress of a television production. A programme may take several months to devise. From the first idea intentions have to be established and after the necessary research a script prepared. Once clarification has taken place and the script has been agreed the programme is cast in a way similar to a theatrical production.

Once the cast has been arranged then rehearsals can start. It is far too expensive to use a studio for the whole time that a production is planned so usually a scripted production will be rehearsed elsewhere before it is committed to the production studio. Time in the studio for an average thirty-minute programme may be about three or four days, depending on the complexity of the programme's structure. Usually the recording is done in one 'take' fairly late on the final day.

We have already studied the way in which the vision mixer can move from camera to camera to select the visual material to be recorded. Below is a description of the basic terms used in this process.

Methods of moving from one shot to another

1. *Cutting*—To cut from one camera to another means to switch directly from one to the other. At an instant the picture from one camera is replaced on the 'transmission' or 'line' monitor (television set) by the picture from a second. This technique is often used during dialogue.
2. *Mixing*—As the picture from one camera fades it is replaced gradually by a picture from a second camera. This change is obtained by moving a sliding switch and its speed can be controlled. It is therefore possible to have either a very slow mix or a fast mix. In the cinema this device is called a 'dissolve'.

Super-Imposition If the mix through from one camera to another is stopped half-way, the result is a combination or over-laying of two images, one from each camera. Very often the day's weather symbols on a weather report map are put on to the basic map by super-imposition. (Fig. 16.)

Wiping In this effect the picture from camera one is superseded by a picture from a second camera which appears to slide up or across the television screen. Special effects generators can do this transition in a number of ways now but such scene changes are usually associated with light entertainment programmes.

So far we have considered the ways in which one visual

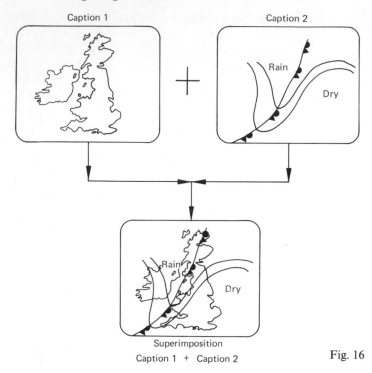

Caption 1

Caption 2

Superimposition
Caption 1 + Caption 2

Fig. 16

image can be replaced by another, In fact the way in which pictures are related together is important.

Look at this extract from *The Film Sense* by Eisenstein (Faber & Faber):

Montage is a mighty aid in the resolution of this task.

Why do we use montage at all? Even the most fanatical opponent of montage will agree that it is not merely because the film strip at our disposal is not of infinite length, and consequently, being condemned to working with pieces of restricted lengths, we have to stick one piece of it on to another occasionally.

The 'leftists' of montage saw it from the opposite extreme. While playing with pieces of film, they discovered a certain property in the toy which kept them astonished for a number of years. This property consisted in the fact *that two film pieces of any kind, placed together, inevitably combine into a new concept, a new quality, arising out of that juxtaposition.*

This is not in the least a circumstance peculiar to the cinema, but is a phenomenon invariably met with in all cases where we have to deal with juxtaposition of two facts, two phenomena, two objects. We are accustomed to make, almost automatically, a definite and obvious deductive generalisation when any separate objects are placed before us side by side. For example, take a grave, juxtaposed with a woman in mourning weeping beside it, and scarcely anybody will fail to jump to the conclusion: *a widow*. It is precisely on this feature of our perception that the following miniature story by Ambrose Bierce bases its effect. It is from his *Fantastic Fables* and is entitled 'The Inconsolable Widow':

A Woman in widow's weeds was weeping upon a grave. 'Console yourself, madam', said a Sympathetic Stranger. Heaven's mercies are infinite. There is another man somewhere, besides your husband, with whom you can still be happy.'
'There was', she sobbed—'there was, but this is his grave.'

The whole effect of this is built upon the circumstance that the grave and the woman in mourning beside it lead to the inference, from established convention, that she is a widow mourning her husband, whereas in fact the man for whom she is weeping is her lover.

The same circumstances is often found in riddles—for example, this one from international folk-lore: 'The raven flew, while a dog sat on its tail. How can this be?' We automatically combine the juxtaposed elements and reduce them to a unity. As a result, we understand the query as though the dog were sitting on the tail of the raven, while actually, the riddle contains two unrelated actions: the raven flies, while the dog sits on its own tail.

This tendency to bring together into a unity two or more independent objects or qualities is very strong, even in the use of separate words, characterising different aspects of some single phenomenon.

We can see that by adding together picture one and picture two we do not just get $1+2$ but an additional factor is involved. This additional factor is provided by the viewer's own construction and response. This can be simply illustrated by placing together two photographs and deciding on the sum total of their expression, linked together.

This juxtaposition of images and the way in which the images are linked together is a very strong tool in the hands of the director. One of his functions is to select camera positions, angles and lens settings to carry out effectively his intention visually, and then link to this the sound.

All the director's decisions about these components of a television programme and how it is to be executed can be recorded in a form of shorthand and is called the camera script. Here is an extract from the script for *You and the World* (Thames Television). It is the opening caption sequence followed by a telecine insert.

You and the World
'The Kick-Off's at Three'

No. 5 by
Michael Cahill

PRODUCER	CHARLES WARREN
Production Assistant	Madge Barnes
Programme Assistant/S.M.	Tony Davenall
Education Officer	Bruce Jamson
Script Editor	Lester Clark
Casting Director	David Asche
Designer	Jim Nicolson
Film Editor	Rosemary MacLoughlin
Advisers	Mrs Elsie Warren/
	Dr Denis Lawton

STUDIO SCHEDULE	
Camera rehearsal	1030–1230
Lunch Break	1230–1330
Camera rehearsal	1330–1530
Tea, Line up, Make-up	1530–1630
VTR	1630–1700
Tech, clear	1700–1715

CREW	
Technical Supervisor	John Eveleigh
Floor Manager	John Cooper
Lighting	Ken Brown
Cameras	Richard Jackman
Sound	Peter Sampson
Racks	Bert White
Vision Mixer	Peter Boffin
Make-up	Pearl Rashbass

VTR: Tuesday, 20 May 1969
Studio 1, Teddington
T/X: June 2/3

RUNNING TIME: 20'00"

CAST
DANNY   Brian Godfrey
TESSA   Diane Grayson
BILLY   Michael Cashman
RENE   Cheryl Hall
DANNY'S MOTHER   Carmel McSharry
UNCLE JOHN   Tommy Godfrey

PERSONS ON FILM
BARRY TURNER   (Voice only)
DANNY   Brian Godfrey
DANNY'S MOTHER   Carmel McSharry
Mr C. Neill, Probation Officer
Juvenile Court in session

FADE UP
1. T/C   16 mm d/h   S.O.F   /
   OPENING IDENT.   (57″)

   10″ T/C BLANKING

2. CUT 3A   CAPTION   /GRAMS: 'STREET GIRL'
   'YOU AND THE WORLD'

3. CUT 4A   CAPTION   /
   'THE KICK-OFF'S AT THREE'
   BY MICHAEL CAHILL
   3 TO B
      FADE MUSIC (@ 26″)

4. CUT T/C (contd) S.O.F.   /TELECINE: CLIP 1
   Danny sitting in a train
   with passengers.   BARRY TURNER
                                  (VOICE OVER FILM):
                              Danny has got things sorted
                              out with Tessa but he still has a
                              lot on his mind.
                                  Tomorrow he appears in the
                              Juvenile Court and he can't help
                              remembering that he's broken
                              the conditions of his probation—
                              and then there's the charge of
                              malicious wounding with an

5. MIX 3B   BOOM A
Uncle cam.L, Danny at
table. Uncle moving
behind to unit.

offensive weapon. All this could
mean that he'll be sent
away. /

UNCLE JOHN'S KITCHEN
JOHN: So you're expecting the
worst at the Juvenile Court
tomorrow then?
DANNY: Yeah . . . I reckon I'll go
away for a while.
JOHN: How's your mother taking
it?
DANNY: She's cut up.

6. CUT 2A
MS John

/JOHN: How do you feel?

7. CUT 1A
MS Danny

/DANNY SHRUGS

8. CUT 2A
MS John

/JOHN: What does that mean?

9. CUT 1A
MS Danny

/DANNY: Fed up!

10. CUT 3B
2-sh as John Xes d/s
to table, clears junk
on table.

/JOHN: How's Tessa?

DANNY: Fine.
JOHN: I got the idea that her
mother and father were the
strict kind from the way she
panicked over that train you
missed. Are they?

JOHN CROSSES U/S

DANNY: They are . . . they
warned her off seeing me. Tessa
left home and her father called
round about it.

11. CUT 2A
MCU John

/JOHN: Why did he do that?

12. CUT 1A
     MCU Danny

/DANNY: He thought I made her do it. He knows about the trouble I'm in.

13. CUT 2A
     MCU John

/JOHN: You can't blame him for getting worked up about it, can you? I suppose he thought he was doing his best by his daughter.

14. CUT 1A   (ON RISE)
     MS Danny. Pan him to sink for 2-sh.

/DANNY: I suppose so, but he blamed me before he knew what had happened. He was only going by what he'd heard about me.
JOHN: All right Danny I know. I know it's not been easy for you at home. I also think you can be difficult—outright obstinate at times. Do you mind my talking to you like this, Danny?
DANNY: I can take it from you Uncle John.
JOHN: Don't waste your life, Danny. Make the most of it, it's precious. Don't let anyone tell you any different.

Pan Uncle John to sink. Danny follows to make 2-sh.

DANNY: I can't see anything precious about it.
JOHN: But you're just starting out in life. There's time.
DANNY: Time for what?
JOHN: For you to think about just what you're doing with your life.

15. CUT 3B
     2-sh. Uncle John
     Xes d/s to table.

/JOHN CROSSES TO TABLE

DANNY: What did you mean about it not being easy for me at home.
JOHN: Well how your Mum and Dad don't get on too well and

Danny helps Uncle
pack things.
Uncle John moves
u/s to cupboard.

how your sisters got more
attention than you did from
your Dad.
DANNY: Everything I did was
always wrong for him.
JOHN: Anyway let's leave it at
that.

16. CUT 1A   /DANNY: Just like Tessa's father.
    MCU Danny   He was only too ready to blame
                           me. Why does it have to be
    3 TO C   me? . . . Why?

17. CUT 2A   /JOHN: Everyone feels like that
    MCU John   when they don't like what's
                           happening to 'em.

18. CUT 1A   /DANNY: I know all about them.
    MCU Danny

19. CUT 2A   /JOHN: Do you?
    MCU John

20. CUT 1A   /DANNY: But I'm talking about
    MCU Danny   myself. Why me?

21. CUT 2A   /JOHN: Everybody says, 'Why
    MCU John   does it have to be me!'

22. CUT 1A   /DANNY: Yeah I know but why
    MS Danny.   me? Others do the same things
    Zoom out to   as I did—even worse and get
    include Uncle.   away with it.

22A. CUT 2A   /JOHN: Yes, but you got caught!
     MCU John   DANNY: I know but you must
                         admit it's not fair.
                         JOHN: That's no excuse for
                         doing what you did. You can't
                         go around breaking the law, go
                         around stealing, smashing things
                         up—doing nothing but damage.

23. CUT 1A   /DANNY XES TO UNCLE

Danny Xes to end of
table. Uncle John   DANNY: I don't mean that!
follows to 2-sh.   JOHN: Well, what do you mean?

2 TO HALL   DANNY: I dunno! Look, I'd
                          better go!
                          DANNY TURNS ON UNCLE,
                          CROSSES, TURNS BACK. UNCLE
                          GOES TO HIM.

                          JOHN: Danny, if you do go
                          away after tomorrow, drop me
                          a line and I shall come and see
                          you, right?
                          DANNY: Thanks a lot Uncle
                          John. Be seeing you.

24. MIX 4A   /BOOM SWING
    2-shot Rene f/g,
    Billy b/g   BILLY'S BEDROOM
                          BILLY: But why should it have
    1 TO B   to be Danny? Others are getting
                          away with it all the time.
                          RENE: You're only saying that
                          because he's your friend, Billy.
                          If he wasn't you'd say, 'Well
                          serves you right mate, you did
                          it now you must pay.' Why
                          should people, because they get
                          excited about things, go around
                          breaking the law, smashing
                          things up, tearing up trains. . . .
                          BILLY: Sometimes you can't help
                          yourself. Sometimes. . . .
                          RENE: Don't give me that.
                          That's no excuse. Remember
                          Danny's been in trouble before,
                          and there was one occasion
                          when she 'got away with it' as
                          you put it. Anyway don't let's
                          go on about it because I'm
                          as upset for him as you are.

BILLY: I agree with you. I
suppose I'm defending him
because I'm his friend and I
don't want him to get into too
much trouble—if only he'd stop
and think sometimes. . . .

All instructions are present. For example in Shot 2 (number at side of the page) the vision mixer has to cut to camera 3 which is at that moment stationed in position A reading a caption entitled 'You and the World'. During this time the sound mixer has put up 'Street Girl' on disc. You will see that this runs for 26 seconds (under Shot 3).

Work through the rest of the extract translating the symbols. Here is an additional glossary to help:

T/C = telecine
16 mm = film size for telecine
S.O.F. = sound over film
10″ = ten seconds
T/C blanking = ten second run-in to telecine film
A, B = denote camera studio positions (3 to B = 3 move to B)
Boom A = sound boom
MS = medium or mid. shot (see previous unit)
2-Sh or 3-Sh etc. = 2 people in shot or 3 people in shot etc.
Xes = crosses
d/s = down-stage

DISCUSSION AND ACTIVITY

1. Devise a plan of a studio based on your own room or acting area. Divide into floor squares (or use graph paper). Using cardboard make scaled cut-outs for apparatus in the studio and use them as templates (see Fig. 18). Measure the amount of room taken up by other items that you may introduce. Figure 19 is an expanded view of the caption illustration. This illustrates camera movements.

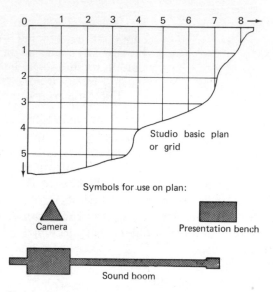

Studio basic plan
or grid

Symbols for use on plan:

Camera

Presentation bench

Sound boom

Devise other shapes by establishing plan-view dimensions

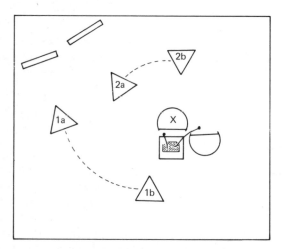

Fig. 19. Expansion of Figure 15 to show initial moves by each camera to new positions. Studio is set for an interview. 1*b* will take in presenter X, giving time for camera 2 to move to 2*b*. Normal studio presentation, for example using five cameras and six sets, is more complicated than this but works on the same principle.

Take an idea for a short television programme—perhaps you can base it on your favourite serial—and first of all devise a script using the shorthand that you have observed. Use your studio plan and plan elevations of studio paraphernalia to work out your script in studio terms. Remember that you must decide between cutting, mixing and wiping.

2. Using a 35 mm camera photograph your production from the angles that you have specified, using correct distances. You will have to tolerate a fixed lens!

3. Produce a sound tape to support your programme effects. Present all this work in a folder including a list of necessary apparatus (microphones etc.) and a description supported by photographs of exterior shots that you may require.

Unit 19

Full, Frontal . . .

The name 'Lord Chamberlain' sounds more appropriate to
pantomime than to serious drama but until recently he
played a very important part in the development of British
theatre. Every play for public performance had to meet the
Lord Chamberlain's requirements:

Any change of title must be submitted for the Lord Chamberlain's approval.

No profanity or impropriety of language to be permitted on the Stage.

No indecency of dress, dance or gesture to be permitted on the Stage.

No objectionable personalities to be permitted on the Stage, nor anything calculated to produce riot or breach of the peace.

No offensive representation of living persons to be permitted on the Stage.

Only on the condition that these were observed was a licence granted in the following terms:

I, the Lord Chamberlain of the Queen's Household for the time being, do by virtue of my Office and in pursuance of powers given to me by the Act of Parliament for regulating Theatres, 6 & 7 Victoria, Cap. 68, Section 12 Allow the Performance of a new Stage Play of which a copy has been submitted to me by you, being a —— in —— Acts. entitled ——— with the exception of the Words and Passages which are specified in the endorsement of the Licence and without further variation whatsoever.

Given under my hand this —— day of —— 19——

Lord Chamberlain

Cuts were frequently ordered in the text for performance when the original was thought blasphemous or offensive to public decency. Fourteen cuts were ordered for John Osborne's *Luther* (see Unit 4) and the use of 'Jesus' as an expletive forbidden in *Mother Courage* (Unit 16). References to royalty were very carefully vetted—the effect on some documentary plays is easy to imagine. Many modern plays contain notes in the published editions listing those parts of the text to be changed in performance: examples include Joe Orton's *Crimes of Passion* (Methuen, 1967) and David Halliwell's *Little Malcolm and his Struggle against the Eunuchs* (French, 1966).

But in 1969 the Lord Chamberlain's role of censor was abolished. One of the results of the gradual liberalising of the L.C.'s attitude and his eventual disappearance has been nudity in serious drama. It is difficult to believe that in 1948 a play *Pick-Up Girl* was refused a licence until the line 'they were both wearing nothing' was deleted.

The rock musical *Hair* (in its sixth year at the time of writing) contains an optional stripping scene; Kenneth Tynan's *Oh Calcutta!* was followed by *Pyjama Tops* in which attractive actresses jumped naked in and out of a transparent swimming pool. The trend has reached Shakespeare: in Bernard Miles's production of *Othello* at the Mermaid Theatre the whole final scene was played by a nude Desdemona. Television has followed the theatre's lead; nudity first appeared in the dramatisation of Hardy's *Jude the Obscure* and Dennis Potter's *Casanova* exploited the naked female form considerably. (At the time of writing a ban on nudity still pertains for the ITA.)

For many years various means of suggesting nudity have been employed: flesh-coloured tights, body stockings and naked shoulders protruding from bed are familiar sights; yet the cinema, subjected as it still is to a form of censorship, has made considerable capital on nudity for some time now.

DISCUSSION

1. On what grounds would you consider nudity a legitimate ingredient of a play?
2. Is there really a connection between nudity and morality?
3. Blasphemy and 'bad' language were also subject to the Lord Chamberlain's cuts. Since the removal of censorship there has been an increase in the use of language described as foul, obscene, filthy, offensive and coarse both in the theatre and on television. It can be argued that since real life includes such language it must inevitably find its way into play texts. Discuss the arguments for and against the use of such language in plays. To what extent must you consider the feelings of the actors and the audience?
4. The nude figure has been a subject for portrayal in painting and sculpture for many centuries. Why do you think that the theatre is the last serious art form to accept the nude in modern times?

5. Bernard Miles justified his nude Desdemona from evidence in the text of the play; he also argued that Shakespeare intended the scene to be played nude even though the part of Desdemona would have been played by a boy! These ideas gave rise to much correspondence in the press: examine the evidence and form your own opinion.

6. The Lord Chamberlain's regulations prevented the impersonation of Christ in the theatre. What is your reaction to *Godspell, Jesus Christ Superstar* and other results of the lifting of this ban?

BIBLIOGRAPHY

Martin Esslin: *Brief Chronicles*, Maurice Temple Smith, London, 1970.
  (The chapter entitled 'Nudity, Barely the Beginning'—to continue the debate.)
Richard Findlater: *Banned*, MacGibbon and Kee, London, 1967.
  (A review of theatrical censorship in Britain.)

Unit 20

'Though Our Lives . . .'?

If you have followed this course you will now be in a position to embark on a more elaborate project.

You will need a copy of Shakespeare's *Macbeth*. Read it with the guidance of your tutor and try to see a production or film of the play.

In Act III Scene i we are introduced to two characters who pose some interesting questions for us, and our work for this unit will be based on your thinking about them. Eventually, it is hoped that you will evolve a substantial piece of drama as a result.

This would not be the first time that two minor characters in one play had stimulated further creative work: Tom Stoppard's play *Rosencrantz and Guildenstern are Dead* stems from Shakespeare's *Hamlet*.

Now study the scenes in which the two murderers appear: Act III Scene i, Act III Scene iii, Act III Scene iv.

1. What do we learn straight away? There had been a previous meeting with Macbeth. What do you think Macbeth had said to them and what was their reaction?

2. In Act III Scene iii they are joined by a third murderer—why? Who was he?

Remember how Stanislavsky encouraged this approach to understanding a character.

Now give the closest possible attention to the text. Don't be content until you have considered every word; then begin to 'build' a character by asking these questions about the murderers:

1. What sort of men do they appear to be by what is said about them?

2. What can we deduce about them from what they say and how they behave?

We come now to the question which has always intrigued the writer: What was the first murderer about to say in Act III Scene i when Macbeth cut in: 'Though our lives . . .'?

Do you think Shakespeare intended any particular completion to this sentence?

Have you any ideas as to what may have happened to the murderers after their final appearance in the play?

After careful consideration of all the questions raised here your activity is as follows:

1. Improvise and eventually script a short play which has an interesting shape and has the murderers as central figures. Include scenes showing (*a*) the earlier interview with Macbeth, (*b*) the plotting and the reaction of wives and friends, (*c*) the original scenes from *Macbeth* rewritten in modern English, (*d*) the result of the murderers' actions.

2. Decide how you will costume the play; rely on effective simplicity and make some props.

3. Stage the play in any way you like but discuss all the possibilities first.

4. Use lighting and make-up if possible.

What remains to make a successful production? This will perhaps form the basis of future work.

Glossary of Theatrical Terms

ACT-DROP   A painted curtain which may be lowered at the end of each act.

ACTING AREA   That part of the stage where actors may move freely in general view of the audience; also an overhead lantern for downward illumination, with a beam and cut-off angle of 25–45 degrees.

AMPERE   The Standard Unit of measurement of electrical current. Cables, fuses and switches are designated by their current-carrying capacity.

APRON   An extension of the stage floor outwards beyond the proscenium towards the audience.

BACKING   Any small scenic piece set behind, and to complete, another piece having an opening, such as a door or window.

BAFFLE   Any sheet of suitable material employed to prevent a spill of light.

BAR   (see BARREL)

BARN-DOOR   (see SHUTTER)

BARREL   A length of iron tubing to which wire or rope lines are attached and which carries any cloth, batten, scenic piece, lighting equipment, etc., so that it may be hauled to or lowered from the grid.

BATTEN   Loosely applied to any length of wood generally found in scenic construction.

BLACK-OUT   The switching off of scene lighting simultaneously and instantly at cue.

BOAT TRUCK   A shallow platform on wheels or castors brought on as a false stage floor having (usually) a revolving part or table incorporated in it.

BOOKFLAT   A pair of hinged flats set like a book upon its edges.

BOOKWING   A hinged wing opened and set similarly to bookflat.

BORDER   Any hanging canvas or material which prevents the audience from seeing out of a scene.

BRACE   A piece of wood introduced diagonally in the frame of a flat to strengthen it, or two strong wood pieces sliding together, capable of being locked and attached to a flat by a hook and used either with a counter-weight on its foot or with a screw in the stage floor, to support the flat.

BRIDGE   That section of the stage floor which by hand, electrical or hydraulic means, may be raised or lowered and retained at a new level. Also a gallery spanning the stage above proscenium height for lighting purposes, effects, tricks, etc.

CLEAT A wooden or iron projection about which a line may be passed and/or made fast.

COLLAPSE Any scenic piece designed to fall in or break up at will.

COLOUR MEDIUM Any translucent material introduced into lantern for colour effects.

CONSOLE A mobile remote control for stage lighting resembling and using certain of the accessories of the cinema organ, e.g. stop keys, keys, pistons, pedals, etc.

CUT-OFF, ANGLE OF The total angle of light from a lantern.

CYCLORAMA A sky cloth which may be curved, hanging usually almost from grid height to the stage floor level; synonymous with panorama or horizon cloth. Sometimes constructed of plywood, cement or sometimes plaster.

DIMMER Any apparatus for decreasing gradually the intensity of lighting, e.g. an electrical resistance.

DIMMER BOARD A switchboard incorporating dimmers.

DRAPERIES Any unspecified material hanging in folds as in scenes or parts of scenes. Specifically velvets, muslins, scrims, casements, woollens, etc.

FALSE PROS (see PROS.)

FIT-UP A combination of diverse arrangements and apparatus for temporary theatrical performances.

FLAT A comprehensive term for any flat piece of scenery, usually of canvas stretched on a frame.

FLIES (FLYS) Galleries running above the stage and at right angles to the pros. from which scenic apparatus is lowered.

FLY To hang anything from the grid on lines over pulleys so that it may be hauled up or flown (see GRID and LINE).

FLY TOWER A space above the stage into which scenery can be raised.

FOOTLIGHTS A row of lamps on the front edge of the stage at floor level and in front of the main curtain. Principal use to neutralise shadows cast by overhead lighting. Known as Magazine footlights when each lamp is in a separate compartment.

GAUZE Used for obscuration. When lit from the front the scene behind is invisible; conversely when unlit the scene behind may be revealed softly. Scenes may be suggested by painting on the gauze itself when front lit; disappearing when lit from behind.

GELATINE (see COLOUR MEDIUM)

GREEN ROOM A meeting room off-stage for the actors.

GRID An arrangement beneath the stage roof, of open slats running parallel to the proscenium opening and carrying pulleys over which lines are rigged from the working flies or convenient positions for hauling scenic apparatus from the stage.

GROUND PLAN A plan of the stage on which is marked the position of scenery.

GROUND ROW Any low piece of scenery running horizontally, or a group of floodlights on the stage floor.

HOUSE LIGHTS The auditorium lighting.

IRIS An adjustable arrangement of flat overlapping leaves in a frame.

Placed in spotlight the beam angle may be altered without changing the focus by varying the amount of overlap.

LIGHTS, CUE   Red and green coloured signal lamps operated from the stage manager's position to appropriate points. Switching gives green to stand by, red to go.

LINNEBACH, ADOLF   (Dresden, stage director for a time.) Inventor of a combined direct/indirect cyclorama floodlight. Also designed and usually associated with a lantern for projecting scenery, using simply a large glass slide in front of light, without any optical system.
NB Only suitable for symbolic effects without accurate definition.

MEZZANINE   The space under the stage.

PERCH   A small platform L. or R. within the pros. opening for an operator with one or more focus lamps and colours.

PROMPT CORNER   The corner of the stage immediately behind the pros. from which the prompter and stage manager direct the performance.

PROPERTY ROOM   The place where the properties are normally stored.

PROS.   A contracted term for proscenium. False Pros.—any complete arched opening for scenery immediately inside the main proscenium arch.

RAIL   The heavy timber or steel edge of the fly gallery.

REVOLVE   A circular revolvable area forming part of the stage floor.

SCENE BAY   The space where scenery is stored and packed.

SCENE DOCK   The space where scenery is generally handled in and out of the theatre, having two narrow, very tall doors.

SET   General term for any complete set of scenery.

SHUTTER   Arrangements of metal leaves for limiting the area of the beams of spot lanterns.

SIGHT LINE   Any imaginary line drawn from any part of the auditorium governing the spectators' view on and off stage.

STRIKE   To dismantle a scene.

TABS   Abbreviation of tableau curtains.

TEASER   A border usually hung between the tormentor wings.

TORMENTOR   Two substantial wings immediately inside the pros. opening, masking the prompt corner.

TRANSPARENCY   Any cloth, hanging or stretched, through which light is caused to produce a specific effect; usually of linen.

TRAP   Any opening cut in the stage floor or scenery and fitted with one or more flaps through which an actor may appear or disappear.

TRUCK   Usually a super-imposed stage platform, sometimes incorporating within itself a REVOLVE (q.v.), capable of being moved on and off stage with or without scenery.